RAISED TOGETHER

A STUDY OF COLOSSIANS

GLORIA FURMAN

LifeWay Press® Nashville, Tennessee

Published by LifeWay Press® • © 2018 Gloria Furman
Reprinted October 2019

ISBN: 978-1-4627-7520-0
Item: 005798099

Dewey Decimal Classification: 227.7
Subject Headings: BIBLE. N.T. COLOSSIANS--STUDY AND TEACHING \ WOMEN \ CHRISTIAN LIFE \ JESUS CHRIST

All Scripture quotations, unless otherwise noted, are taken from The Holy Bible, English Standard Version® (ESV®), copyright © 2001 by Crossway, a publishing ministry of Good News Publishers. Used by permission. All rights reserved. Scripture quotations marked CSB® are taken from the Christian Standard Bible®, Copyright © 2017 by Holman Bible Publishers. Used by permission. Christian Standard Bible® and CSB® are federally registered trademarks of Holman Bible Publishers. Scripture quotations marked KJV are from the Holy Bible, King James Version.

To order additional copies of this resource, order online at www.lifeway.com; write LifeWay Christian Resources Customer Service: One LifeWay Plaza, Nashville, TN 37234; fax order to 615.251.5933; or call toll-free 1.800.458.2772.
Printed in the United States of America

Adult Ministry Publishing
LifeWay Resources
One LifeWay Plaza
Nashville, TN 37234

PRODUCTION TEAM

Author:
Gloria Furman

Content Editor:
Elizabeth Hyndman

Video Producer
& Director:
Rick Simms

Editorial Manager:
Michelle Hicks

Production Editor:
Lindsey Bush

Art Director:
Heather Wetherington

Director, LifeWay
Adult Ministry:
Faith Whatley

CONTENTS

ABOUT THE AUTHOR

Gloria Furman is a wife, mother of four, and writer. In 2008, her family moved to the Middle East to plant Redeemer Church of Dubai where her husband, Dave, serves as the pastor. She is the author of several books including *Treasuring Christ When Your Hands Are Full*, *Missional Motherhood*, *Alive in Him*, and the *Missional Motherhood Bible Study*.

A NOTE FROM GLORIA

Hello!

Greetings from the sandy Arabian Peninsula. The sun is setting over this desert city tonight, and I'm reminded of friends and family who are just waking up on the other side of the world. As this terrestrial ball rolls around the sun, I often think of these lines from the hymn "The Day Thou Gavest, Lord, Is Ended," by John Ellerton, about the melody of unceasing praise the Lord receives from His church across the globe:

> We thank Thee that Thy church, unsleeping,
> While earth rolls onward into light,
> Through all the world her watch is keeping,
> And rests not now by day or night.
> As o'er each continent and island
> The dawn leads on another day,
> The voice of prayer is never silent,
> Nor dies the strain of praise away.

"From the rising of the sun to its setting, let the name of the LORD be praised" (Ps. 113:3, CSB). Jesus is worthy of unceasing praise! I'm excited to walk with you through Paul's letter to the church at Colossae and learn more about Jesus and how He reigns supreme over the cosmos. What a glorious vocation we have been given—to praise Jesus together—because we have been raised together with Christ.

In Christ,

Gloria

HOW TO USE THIS STUDY

Welcome to *Raised Together*! This eight-session Bible study can be used in a number of settings. It's primarily designed to be used in a weekly small group with a leader and a small gathering of women. However, the study can also be used as an individual study, in a one-on-one discipling relationship, or with a large group of women.

STUDY ELEMENTS

GROUP SESSION

During the Group Session you will discuss and process together what you are learning through the video teaching and the Personal Study time. Each Group Session will consist of four parts:

REVIEW: A list of questions will help you assess and discuss what you've studied in your Personal Study.

WATCH: Following the review, you'll watch the video teaching for the session. Space is provided for you to take notes on the teaching.

DISCUSS: Review and process the video teaching as a group, using the questions provided.

CLOSE: A suggested final prayer prompt or activity closes the Group Session.

PERSONAL STUDY

There are five Personal Study sections each week. This material will give you an opportunity to dig deeper into Paul's Letter to the Colossians as well as preview the teaching video in the coming session. You can complete these Personal Study sections at your own pace. However, it would probably be best to space them out through the week to give you time to ponder God's Word and how to apply it.

ABOUT THE GOSPEL COALITION

The Gospel Coalition is a fellowship of evangelical churches deeply committed to renewing our faith in the gospel of Christ and to reforming our ministry practices to conform fully to the Scriptures. We have become deeply concerned about some movements within traditional evangelicalism that seem to be diminishing the church's life and leading us away from our historic beliefs and practices. On the one hand, we are troubled by the idolatry of personal consumerism and the politicization of faith; on the other hand, we are distressed by the unchallenged acceptance of theological and moral relativism. These movements have led to the easy abandonment of both biblical truth and the transformed living mandated by our historic faith. We not only hear of these influences—we see their effects. We have committed ourselves to invigorating churches with new hope and compelling joy based on the promises received by grace alone through faith alone in Christ alone.

We believe that in many evangelical churches a deep and broad consensus exists regarding the truths of the gospel. Yet we often see the celebration of our union with Christ replaced by the age-old attractions of power and affluence, or by monastic retreats into ritual, liturgy, and sacrament. What replaces the gospel will never promote a mission-hearted faith anchored in enduring truth working itself out in unashamed discipleship eager to stand the tests of kingdom-calling and sacrifice. We desire to advance along the King's highway, always aiming to provide gospel advocacy, encouragement, and education so that current and next-generation church leaders are better equipped to fuel their ministries with principles and practices that glorify the Savior and do good to those for whom He shed His life's blood.

We want to generate a unified effort among all peoples—an effort that is zealous to honor Christ and multiply His disciples, joining in a true coalition for Jesus. Such a biblically grounded and united mission is the only enduring future for the church. This reality compels us to stand with others who are stirred by the conviction that the mercy of God in Jesus Christ is our only hope of eternal salvation. We desire to champion this gospel with clarity, compassion, courage, and joy—gladly linking hearts with fellow believers across denominational, ethnic, and class lines.

Our desire is to serve the church we love by inviting all our brothers and sisters to join us in an effort to renew the contemporary church in the ancient gospel of Christ so we truly speak and live for Him in a way that clearly communicates to our age. As pastors, we intend to do this in our churches through the ordinary means of His grace: prayer, ministry of the Word, baptism and the Lord's Supper, and the fellowship of the saints. We yearn to work with all who seek the lordship of Christ over the whole of life with unabashed hope in the power of the Holy Spirit to transform individuals, communities, and cultures.

SESSION 1:

INTRODUCTION

Ice Breaker: Either /or · 5 personal study

GROUP TIME REVIEW

Welcome to Session 1 of *Raised Together*! My hope is that God would use this Bible study to grow your love for Jesus and strengthen your faith as you live for Him. Colossians is a letter written by the apostle Paul to the church at Colossae nearly two thousand years ago. But you aren't reading other peoples' mail, so don't worry. Colossians is God's Word, and it is for everyone.

Before we begin this study on Colossians, take some time to get to know the ladies with whom you are studying.

Share your name and a little information about yourself and/or your family.

Share what drew you to this study.

Describe your familiarity with Colossians.

Colossians is all about Jesus. What have you heard about Him? How does the person and work of Jesus impact your life today?

WATCH VIDEO ON INTRODUCTION TO COLOSSIANS

DISCUSS INTRODUCTION TO COLOSSIANS VIDEO

What are some of the questions you are excited to hear more about as we study Colossians together?

What does it mean to be "raised together" with Christ and other believers?

Gloria shared part of her story in this video. What's your story? How would you describe your journey of faith?

_____

_____

_____

_____

_____

_____

_____

_____

_____

_____

_____

_____

_____

_____

_____

_____

_____

CLOSE

Break into small groups and spend time praying with one another. Ask God to bless your study of His Word and your fellowship with each other as you embark on this study of Colossians together.

SESSION 2:
COLOSSIANS
1:1-14

ONE

Welcome to your Personal Study time. In the group session we talked about the need to understand the nature of Paul's Letter to the Colossians and how we should approach it. How is the letter organized? Why is it here? What is the message of the letter? How should we live in light of what we learn? These questions and their answers are critical for us to understand, because our primary goal in this study of Colossians is to know God.

In our study of Colossians we are interacting with the very Word of God, so let's pray together for His help.

> Father in heaven, we are Your humble creatures. You've created us to be dependent on Your Word. We know You have made us to live by "every word that comes from the mouth of the LORD" (Deut. 8:3). We confess to You, Lord, that we forget this truth so often and we attempt to live apart from Your Word. Forgive us. Would Your Holy Spirit cause our hearts to burn with zeal for Your Word? Only with Your help can we understand Your Word in Colossians. Help us to read, understand, and apply Colossians to the glory of Your Son Jesus. It is in His name we pray, Amen.

This week we are going to cover the introduction of Paul's Letter to the Colossians. You will notice that these fourteen verses really pack a lot in there!

In this initial Personal Study this week, please read through the whole letter of Colossians. If you are able, read through all four chapters in one sitting. If you are reading the translation of Scripture you are most comfortable with, this should only take about fifteen minutes. Once you are finished reading, if you have more time for another read through (whether right now or later), read through the whole letter in one sitting again. In the course of our study we will examine Colossians in different proportions—from chapters to paragraphs to verses to words. All of this will be done in light of the whole, which is a single letter.

After your initial read through of Colossians, take a few minutes to write a couple of notes below about what stood out to you.

Paul's concern for people he had never met. He had only "heard" of them

Epaphras was converted by Paul and Epaphras brought the gospel to Colossae

Reminds the Colossae who Jesus was an what He did for them.

The letter speaks to their identity in Christ.

[colostrum milk (breast)]

Church at Colossae was mostly Gentiles 1:21

workplace behavior

Very encouraging

Specific instructions for living Holy

Reminding of Christ's sacrifice

TWO

For the rest of the week we will go in-depth into Colossians 1:1-14. We will also be looking up some cross-references in the Old Testament and the other parts of the New Testament, though, to help us better understand the context. But before we do, let's recall what we've already read. Since we've already read the whole letter, let's review some general questions.

What impressed you about this letter during your read through(s)?

What is the main message Paul is conveying in this letter?

How has Paul organized his letter? Which particular parts can you identify (greetings, prayers, instructions, etc.)?

SLOWLY READ THROUGH COLOSSIANS 1:1-14, PAUL'S INTRODUCTORY GREETING AND PRAYER. *There are several key words and themes in these first fourteen verses that are expounded upon throughout the rest of the letter.*

What are the key words/themes you notice in this passage?

This letter is from Paul and was likely written by the hand of "Timothy our brother," who was acting as Paul's secretary (Col. 1:1). Paul identifies himself as "an apostle of Christ Jesus by the will of God."

Whom does Paul identify as the recipients of this letter?

Colossae is a geographic location one can point to on a map. What is the meaning of the location "in Christ"?

Do you understand yourself to be "in Christ"? Explain.

SLOWLY READ VERSE 3 A FEW TIMES, MEDITATING ON EACH WORD. At first glance, these initial comments from Paul may not seem at all contentious, especially if one is accustomed to hearing Jesus referred to as the Son of God.

Why is it important that Paul says he is thanking "God, the Father of our Lord Jesus Christ"?

What does this mean for our friends, family, and neighbors who deny that God is the Father of the Lord Jesus Christ?

READ PAUL'S REMARKS ON THOSE WHO DENY GOD IN ROMANS 1:21.

This dark and grave depiction of those who are outside of Christ is no longer true of the saints and faithful brothers in Christ at Colossae. And it is no longer true for any and all who are in Christ. Praise God! The futility of our thinking has been replaced by the mind of Christ (1 Cor. 2:16) and our darkened, foolish hearts have been replaced with hearts of flesh.

NOW READ EZEKIEL 36:26.

This is God's work in our lives. We did not do a single thing to merit such a gift! You could say that the only thing we contributed to our salvation is that we desperately needed it. If you are a believer in Christ Jesus, take some time right now to praise God specifically for your salvation in Christ.

Recall the time when you did not know the Lord—your thinking was futile and your heart was darkened. Remember when the light "turned on" for you. What's your born again birth story? What were the circumstances? Who was the messenger God sent to you? What was that day like?

If you came to know Jesus at a very young age, praise the Lord for His miraculous grace in your life. No one who has been delivered from the domain of darkness and transferred to the kingdom of God's beloved Son could possibly have a "boring" born again birth story!

Write a prayer of thanks to God, the Father of our Lord Jesus Christ, for delivering you.

_____

_____

_____

_____

_____

_____

_____

_____

_____

_____

_____

_____

_____

_____

_____

_____

_____

_____

_____

If you are not yet a Christian, and you are investigating the claims of Jesus, I am so glad you are doing this study on Colossians. My prayer for you is that in the days and weeks to come, that "God, who said, 'Let light shine out of darkness,'" will show "in our hearts to give the light of the knowledge of the glory of God in the face of Jesus Christ" (2 Cor. 4:6).

As we continue to study Colossians together, no doubt you will see the glory of God in the face of Jesus Christ. Make it your ongoing prayer that God's Holy Spirit would open the eyes of your heart. I pray you would be raised from death to life through faith in the powerful working of God.

THREE

One of the brilliant by-products of globalization is the ease of communication. I believe that God has strategically designed all of the comings and goings of every people group under the sun. He has done this for the spread of His glorious gospel and in such a way as to bring glory to His Son. The residents of Colossae were beneficiaries of this ease of communication. Ancient Colossae was a small city near a meandering river in the Lycus Valley, but its proximity to the port city of Ephesus allowed opportunities for the exchange of information. Epaphras was a local man who went on a journey to Ephesus and came back with good news for his people—the good news of the gospel! This, of course, was no surprise to the sovereign God, who planned it all before the foundation of the world.

Paul's thanksgiving and prayer in this passage reveal so much to us about "the word of the truth, the gospel" (Col. 1:5). Indeed, the entire letter teaches us about the gospel. *But what is the gospel?* One of the things that potential members of our church are asked to do in their "membership chat" with an elder is to summarize the gospel briefly. The elders are not looking for a perfectly-memorized treatise, but a faithful explanation of the good news of Jesus Christ.

> *Can you summarize the gospel? Try to summarize the good news in less than one hundred words. It is helpful to keep in mind these four things as you write your summary: our holy God, man's rebellion, the sacrifice of Jesus, and the response that is required of us all.*

READ COLOSSIANS 1:1-14, LOOKING CAREFULLY AT VERSES 3-8.

What do we learn about the gospel from this passage of Scripture?

There are certainly many aspects of the word of truth we could discuss at this point. I do want to point out verse 6 right now. It sounds rather astonishing, doesn't it? Paul specifically describes the gospel as that "which has come to you [the Colossians], as indeed in the whole world it is bearing fruit and increasing." The whole world! Bearing fruit and increasing! Now, when we read the newspaper or scroll through a newsreel on the news app in our phones, we are not likely to read such encouraging words. We are more likely to encounter horrific headlines that can tie one's stomach into knots, make the blood boil, or induce anxiety. This news, however, that the gospel is bearing fruit and increasing in the whole world, is exceptionally encouraging and increases our faith.

We ought not be surprised, though. This is what God had planned from before time. In Genesis 12 He reveals more specifically His promise to bless the whole world. We read about the covenant God made with Abram (who would become Abraham) in Genesis 17:7 that God would bless the nations of the earth through the "offspring" ("seed," KJV) of Abraham. Through Abraham's son, Isaac, came the nation of Israel. Isaac and Israel typologically fulfilled God's promise, *and* they pointed ahead to Jesus Christ, who is the ultimate fulfillment of God's promise to bless every nation.

READ MATTHEW 1:1.

Matthew wants his Jewish readers to recognize Jesus. Who does Matthew intentionally identify Jesus with in this passage?

NOW SKIP AHEAD TO MATTHEW 28:18-20.

As the seed of Abraham, Jesus has been shown to be the heir of the covenant God made with Abraham. Which nations are included when Jesus tells His disciples to go make more disciples?

SLOWLY READ GALATIANS 3:7-22, AND THEN CIRCLE BACK TO GALATIANS 3:7-9.

Who are the sons of Abraham? What is the means by which the Christians at Colossae (Gentiles!) are included as sons of Abraham?

Paul had not carried the gospel to Colossae and delivered it in person, but Epaphras heard the good news in Ephesus and brought it back to his friends, family, and neighbors in Colossae. Paul isn't bragging about his ministry when he says the gospel is bearing fruit and increasing in the whole world. His words describe a hallmark of the gospel—its universality.

The word of truth is universally applicable to every man, woman, and child everywhere, and it is the power of God to save any and all who call on Him in faith. The gospel is never adjusted for any people group, as this adjusted news would actually become a totally different false gospel. False gospels (heresies) take on the nuances from the cultures in which they originate, but the true gospel belongs to God (Rom. 1:1-3) and is universal truth.

And so, the word of truth, the gospel, has also come to you. As the beautiful feet of messengers run throughout the world with the good news, God is keeping His covenant with Abraham to bless the world through his offspring—through Christ. Isaiah prophesied,

The people who walked in darkness have seen a great light; those who dwelt in a land of deep darkness, on them has light shown.
ISAIAH 9:2

This is the news headline we need to recall as we go about our days and nights. If you are discouraged right now and have a hard time believing that God is not slow to fulfill His promises (2 Pet. 3:9), ask your friends at church about what God is doing in their lives to get a taste of the increasing, fruit-bearing work of the gospel. Watch films about the spread of the gospel in other lands.

Can you see your own role in this wonderful tapestry of God's blessing of the whole world? Isn't it marvelous that God has sent us His Son! I am amazed afresh at the great patience of God to fulfill His promise to Abraham (even as He continues to be faithful to His covenant). Do you know the "Epaphras" who brought you the word of truth? Who are the people in your life to whom God is sending you with the good news? He could be sending you down a river like Epaphras, across the kitchen to a family member, across the office to a coworker, or …?

Take some time today to pray for the people in your life who do not yet believe the word of truth. Are you in contact with any of the missionaries your church supports? Perhaps you could connect with them and take note of their specific prayer requests during this current season and pray for them. Use the space below to write down the names of people whom you are praying for and your prayers for them.

FOUR

No doubt, as you read through the entire Letter of Colossians earlier in the week you noticed some major themes rise to the forefront. One of those themes is the knowledge of God. What is the knowledge of God? How can we get it? How do we know we have it? Or have enough of it?

Possessing the knowledge of God is very different than possessing the knowledge of multiplication tables or how to drive a car. If you have ever tried to learn a foreign language, you've probably been puzzled by the verbs and their usage when it comes to "knowing" things. One time I asked one of my foreign language tutors to explain to me how I could know when to use one verb over the other when it comes to "knowing" something, and even she was puzzled! "I cannot explain it to you, I think you just have to know," she said, and then we both cracked up laughing.

SLOWLY READ THROUGH PAUL'S PRAYER IN COLOSSIANS 1:9-14.
(Sometimes it's tricky to follow along when you read Paul's prayers, so just read it through a few more times if you get stuck in any of the multiple commas in those phrases.)

What are Paul's specific prayer requests in these verses?

What do you think is the connection between the Colossians being "filled with the knowledge of [God's] will in all spiritual wisdom and understanding" (v. 9) and the rest of the prayer requests?

According to verse 10, how does one "walk in a manner worthy of the Lord"?

Why does Paul ask that they be "strengthened with all power, according to [God's] glorious might" (v. 11)?

Does any of this seem overwhelming to you? In what way?

Most of us are woefully aware of our own inadequacies. I could easily give you a list of all the ways I have mismanaged my time, stopped short of reaching a goal, misunderstood instructions that were given to me, or simply gone to bed early because I couldn't envision myself having the energy to do one more thing. We are fragile, human creatures. Last I checked, transforming into a superhero was not on the list of spiritual gifts given to the church by the ascended Christ. We do not shed our creaturely humanness when we become Christians. Where does our sufficiency come from? It comes from Christ Himself. Paul prays for these things because we so desperately need them. Remember, remember, remember—don't ever forget it—we are in Christ! These blessings are ours in Christ.

The knowledge of God's will is ours in Christ. We can "walk in a manner worthy of the Lord" and be "fully pleasing to him," because we are in Christ (Col. 1:10). We can bear "fruit in every good work" and increase "in the knowledge of God," because we are in Christ. Amen?

Wait. Have you read this somewhere before? Think way back to the beginning of the Bible. If you have read Genesis before, do you recall a story from around creation-time about mankind bearing fruit/increasing and the knowledge that belongs to God?

READ GENESIS 1:26-28.

In whose image did God create mankind (male and female)?

What did God say when He blessed the man and the woman He created?

NOW READ GENESIS 2:16-17.

What does God command the man not to do? What are the consequences of disobedience to God's command?

AND NOW READ GENESIS 3:2-3.

What is the difference between God's command (Gen. 2:16-17) and what the woman says to the serpent?

It cannot be overstated that being made in God's image is profoundly connected to knowing God and knowing His will. Adam and Eve were created in God's image and given the task of multiplying into more godly image bearers. But they sinfully desired to enjoy a particular insight apart from God (the knowledge of good and evil), and when tempted with an opportunity to take this knowledge for themselves, they sank their teeth into the forbidden fruit. The knowledge of God's will had already been made plain to them by God Himself, but the man and the woman disobeyed. In their quest for this special wisdom, they showed that they were fools. From that moment on, everyone born of Adam and Eve has been born spiritually dead—apart from God, their Creator. And every person born is in need of a Mediator to stand between them and the righteous wrath of God.

Paul prays that the Colossians (and us) would "be filled with the knowledge of his will in all spiritual wisdom and understanding" (Col. 1:9). We don't need some new, better knowledge of God, but we need to be filled with all that is ours to have in Christ. We don't need some secret, exclusive knowledge of God, but we need to understand how to obey God's will. We need discernment to appropriate God's will for our lives. It is utterly ironic, isn't it? In their quest for God's knowledge, Adam and Eve failed to apply the knowledge of God to their lives. We do the same thing, too. Oh Father, forgive us!

But now we are in Christ! In Christ we may be filled with the knowledge of God's will in all spiritual wisdom and understanding, and that's the only way Colossians 1:10 can happen in our lives.

Read the following passages where Jesus describes His mission. Make a note of what Jesus says He is concerned with doing.

John 4:34

John 6:38

Luke 22:42

NOW READ COLOSSIANS 1:9-10 ONCE MORE.

Recall how our first parents were given the charge to be fruitful and multiply into more godly image bearers who live by God's Word and obey God's will. How did Jesus perfectly live out verses 9-10?

How is Jesus "the last Adam" (1 Cor. 15:45), through His church, doing what the first Adam failed to do?

Praise God for giving us His Son! What a thrill it is to be placed in Christ and to have all that is in Him. The knowledge of God's will, the ability to bear fruit in every good work, to be strengthened with all power, to endure patiently with joy— thank You, Father, for qualifying us to share in the inheritance of the saints in light.

Pray through Paul's prayer to close your Personal Study time today, personalizing it for yourself and others in your life.

FIVE

Well, we are only about fourteen verses in to Paul's Letter to the Colossians, and we've been all the way back to God's plan of salvation from before time, up to the creation, and all the way forward to the spread of the ever-fruitful, ever-increasing gospel over the whole world. All of this is going somewhere. We are headed for the day when we will be delivered, once and for all, from all futility and pain and even from death itself. It is the "day of redemption" for which we have been sealed by the promised Holy Spirit (Eph. 4:30).

Paul said that he has not ceased to pray for the church at Colossae, and he lists out what he is praying for. We've seen that being placed in Christ is the reason we can avail of these tremendous things—things like spiritual wisdom, fruitful ministry, and spiritual strength. We recall in Colossians 1:11 the strength Paul is praying for comes via the glorious might of God, and it is for all endurance and patience with joy. My kindergarten-aged son likes to imagine he has powers that can enable him to punch through cement walls. Some of us bigger kids like to pretend we have special powers that enable us to do things like consume everything we can (fiscally or otherwise), be exempt from things like sleep and fellowship, and ignore our needs to pray and meditate on God's Word. But as we are filled with the knowledge of God's will in all spiritual wisdom and understanding, we learn to discern what we really need and why.

According to verse 11, why do you need all endurance? Why do you need patience? What kind of patience do you need?

The One who is doing the work requested in this prayer is God, and we are the ones who need endurance and patience with joy. God is the One who fills us with knowledge, enables us to walk in a worthy manner, bears fruit through us, strengthens us, and qualifies us to share in the inheritance of the saints in light. There is something else that God has done for us that Paul wants us to recall.

READ VERSES 13-14.

What has God done for us?

In whom do we have redemption and the forgiveness of sins?

In the Old Testament, when God's people sinned greatly against God time and again, one of the most devastating consequences was the judgment of being exiled out of the promised land and into captivity in foreign nations. God spoke through His prophets time and again to remind His people of His faithfulness to keep His promises. He promised He would bring them out of exile—out of captivity. The promise of deliverance was initially fulfilled when God did bring the nation of Israel out of exile and back to the land He had given to them. But the ultimate fulfillment of God's promise of deliverance—often called the second exodus—is fulfilled when Christ, through His work on the cross, redeems His people from their exile in Satan's kingdom and their bondage to sin. In the Book of Isaiah, we read some truly captivating descriptions of God's redemption of His people from exile.

READ ISAIAH 44:22-24.

What do you notice about redemption and the forgiveness of sins?

NOW READ ISAIAH 52.

What powerful imagery stands out to you in this passage as it pertains to redemption and forgiveness?

As there are echoes in this Colossians passage of God's redemption of His people out of exile, there are also echoes of the exodus of God's people out of slavery in Egypt. Specifically, Paul uses the dark and light imagery to help the readers see the connection.

Go through these passages in Exodus and make notes of the dark and light imagery.

Exodus 10:21-23

Exodus 14:20

While we, God's people, are not corporately going through a literal exodus from one geographic place to another, we are going through a spiritual exodus from the domain of darkness to the kingdom of God's beloved Son. In Luke 22:53, Jesus says these words to the soldiers as He is betrayed by Judas and allows Himself to be arrested (and later executed on the cross), "When I was with you day after day in the temple, you did not lay hands on me. But this is your hour, and the power of darkness." In a glorious irony, in order to deliver us from the kingdom of darkness, Jesus willingly subjected Himself to the power of darkness. Three days later Jesus is shown to be victorious over Satan, sin, and death as He bursts from the grave, the first man in the new creation. And like Him, we will rise! We're delivered spiritually at first, and then in the final resurrection we are delivered in totality. We belong to the kingdom of God's beloved Son even now, and our inheritance is guaranteed; yet we are waiting for the day of redemption when Christ's kingdom will come in full, and we will obtain the inheritance of the saints in light. All of this—deliverance, transferring of citizenship, redemption, forgiveness of sins—is accomplished for us by Christ on our behalf.

Do you actively hope (Col. 1:5) in the things Paul discusses in these verses? If not, what are some ways you can remind yourself to have hope in Christ and His work?

Would you consider yourself to be delivered from darkness, redeemed,
and forgiven by God? If so, what are some of the temptations you face that
cause you to doubt or forget these truths? If not, what assurances do you
find in this passage in Colossians that these things are possible for you
because of Christ?

Acts 13:38-39 says, "Therefore, let it be known to you, brothers and sisters, that
through this man forgiveness of sins is being proclaimed to you. Everyone who
believes is justified through him from everything that you could not be justified
from through the law of Moses" (CSB). Jesus purchased our redemption from sin
at the cost of His own blood on the cross. Jesus canceled our debt, and therefore,
we are pardoned for our sin!

Reflecting on Colossians 1:1-14, what does this new freedom look like in the
life of a believer?

Looking back over verses 13-14, and keeping in mind the whole message
of Colossians, what do you think are some of the reasons that Paul wants
his readers to see and understand their connection with Jesus—the fact
that they are now "in Christ"?

Praise the God and Father of our Lord Jesus Christ! We have so much to be
thankful for, and so many things to pray for ourselves, for our loved ones, and
for the billions of unreached people who do not even know the name of Jesus.
Praise God today for the work He has done and is doing in your life and for the
work He is doing as His fruit-bearing, ever-increasing gospel goes throughout the
whole world. And let's look forward to gathering together to fellowship around
the Word of God.

GROUP TIME REVIEW

Welcome to the Session 2 group time of *Raised Together*! Let's begin by reviewing your Personal Study from the past week.

What is the main message of Colossians?

What are the key words and themes in Colossians?

What does it mean to be "in Christ"? In whom were we before we were placed in Christ? How has God placed us in Christ?

What is the gospel?

What is the connection between being made in God's image and knowing God's will?

_____

_____

_____

_____

_____

_____

_____

_____

_____

_____

_____

_____

_____

_____

_____

_____

_____

WATCH VIDEO ON COLOSSIANS 1:1-14

DISCUSS VIDEO ON COLOSSIANS 1:1-14

What does the apostle Paul want the Colossians (and us) to know?

Why is this message a matter of eternal life and death?

What is the means by which Paul communicates this important truth in Colossians?

Who are the Epaphrases among you? (Hint: The answer is all of you who have heard and obeyed the good news!) What are some of the challenges you face in sharing the gospel with people in your community? How does this text encourage you?

We are all prone to wander away from the purity of the gospel. What are some of the ways you (and those in your community) are tempted to add to the gospel or detract from it? How does this passage in Colossians correct such thinking?

_____

_____

_____

_____

_____

_____

_____

_____

_____

CLOSE

We are all indebted to the grace of God in sending His Son, Jesus. Let's close in prayer together now, thanking the God and Father of our Lord Jesus Christ for loving us in this way—even while we were still sinners. Thank Him for delivering you from the kingdom of darkness and transferring you into the kingdom of His beloved Son. Pray that those who do not yet believe would behold the light of the knowledge of God's glory in the face of Jesus Christ.

SESSION 3:
COLOSSIANS 1:15-23

ONE

Welcome to your Personal Study of Colossians 1:15-23. Last week we studied the introductory remarks and prayer in this letter from Paul to the church at Colossae. He addressed his letter to the saints in Christ at Colossae, who are faithful brothers and sisters. We learned that our saintliness and faithfulness are not owing to anything we have done, but are owing to the fact that we are in Christ. Paul thanked God, the Father of our Lord Jesus Christ, for the obvious, indisputable, and wonderful work He was doing by His Spirit in the Colossian believers. Paul prayed that these faithful brothers and sisters would be filled with the knowledge of God's will, which wasn't some new knowledge they didn't already know. They already had the gospel, which had been faithfully preached to them by one of their own, Epaphras. Paul's prayer, rather, is that they would be filled with this word of truth, which they had already believed. He prayed they would live out the truth of their new identification—they were now new creations in Christ and were to have faith, love, and hope in accordance with that knowledge and be spiritually fruitful.

In Colossians 1:4-5 we read about the evidences of God's love in the Colossians' lives. What is Exhibit A, so to speak, of the evidences of God's love?

How have you seen this evidence exhibited in your own life?

We learned we are all prone to wander away from the purity of the gospel, just like our brothers and sisters at Colossae. We may not be facing the exact same false teaching or empty deceit according to human traditions, but we are indeed facing lies that are not according to Christ. We don't want to be taken captive by these things and led away from following Christ. We learned in the first verses of this letter that Paul's chief strategy in combating these challenges that faced the Colossian church was to highlight, describe, and explain the supremacy of Jesus Christ. Over and over again, Paul exalts Christ, and he calls to his readers' minds the fact of their new identification with Christ.

How is this an effective strategy for combating falsehoods about who God is, who we are, and the person and work of Christ?

Name one or two specific lies about God, Jesus, or yourself by which you are vulnerable to being taken captive.

How does the truth about Christ and your identification with Him nullify those lies?

READ FROM ROMANS 8:

Now in this hope we were saved, but hope that is seen is not hope, because who hopes for what he sees? Now if we hope for what we do not see, we eagerly wait for it with patience.
ROMANS 8:24-25, CSB

In Colossians 1:5 Paul commends the faith and love the Colossians have "because of the hope laid up for you in heaven." Last week we discussed our distinctly Christian hope and our need for endurance and patience with joy.

People hope in a lot of things. What exactly is our distinctly Christian hope?

Describe your own feelings of hope right now—what are you hoping for?

How does the hope of unhindered fellowship with God help you wait patiently for complete redemption in the future?

The passage we are going to study this week is Colossians 1:15-23. These lines have been described as an ancient hymn. Read through Colossians 1:15-23 slowly five times, meditating on each word. If you are so inclined, try singing verses 15-20 (even if you feel you are not gifted musically). Take time to pray through this passage, worshiping Jesus for who He is and praising God for the work He has done, which is described in verses 21-23.

TWO

We could spend a lifetime studying these verses! In view of the themes of Colossians, we recognize that acquiring mere knowledge cultivates arrogance, whereas the knowledge of God produces in us a love for God and others. Let's pray for God's help as we get started.

God and Father of our Lord Jesus Christ, thank You for who You are. You never change. Thank You for Your Son. The only way I can have fellowship with You is through Him. Thank You. God, would Your Holy Spirit now help me as I read Your Word today. Give me insight and clarity of thought so that I can understand the meaning of Your Word as You intend it. Incline my heart to love You with all my heart, mind, soul, and strength, and to love my neighbor as I love myself. In Jesus' name, Amen.

READ THROUGH COLOSSIANS 1:15-23 A COUPLE OF TIMES.

What stands out to you in these verses?

Are there any words that are unfamiliar to you? What phrases seem difficult to understand? List them out.

Did you notice the natural division into two parts in this text? How would you summarize both of these sections in your own words?

There is no other god besides God. And God is the Father of our Lord Jesus Christ. To deny that Jesus is the Son of God is to deny God. Both the Father and the Son are God. The logic of this is simple enough for a child to understand and yet divisive enough to split the most intimate of friends and family members. In some countries there are mothers who report their Christian daughters to the police. Fathers may have their Christian sons executed. Employers may fire Christian employees without just cause. Neighbors can harass Christian neighbors without repercussions. Christian students can be mocked in school. Although millions and millions of people around the world are willing to sit in coffee shops together and happily acknowledge that Jesus was a historical figure, to testify to the deity of Jesus Christ brings "antisocial" consequences— to put it mildly. Many people bestow on Jesus respectful titles, such as "prophet of God" or "wise teacher," but there is an "only" attached to these descriptions in their confession and their allegiance. Christians, however, declare with joy that Jesus is the One and Only Son of God—the image of the invisible God. We worship Jesus and follow His supreme leadership.

With all that said, now let's take a close look at verse 15: "He is the image of the invisible God, the firstborn of all creation."

At first glance, what do you think this sentence means? What do you think it doesn't mean? Why?

It is significant to note that Paul is not picking up a new train of thought at the theology train station in this verse. He is further developing the thoughts he has previously announced in the verses before this one. Quickly glance back to Colossians 1:13-14. Can you see how Paul is explaining who this "beloved Son" is who has accomplished redemption and forgiveness of sins?

According to verse 15, what qualifies Jesus as the One who is able to accomplish redemption for His people and purchase the forgiveness of their sins?

In order to understand what Paul means by Christ being the image of God here in verse 15, it helps to see how this term is used elsewhere in his letters and in other passages in Scripture. Read the following verses to help establish some more background for this idea. Make note of key phrases that describe Jesus in each passage.

John 1:1-3 WORD

Romans 8:29 FIRSTBORN

2 Corinthians 4:4 TRUTH   IMAGE of GOD

1 Corinthians 15:45-49 - LAST ADAM

Philippians 2:5-8

Hebrews 1:1-4

One would think that in light of the evidence that Jesus Christ is God, we would be wholeheartedly convinced He is the only One who is able to accomplish our redemption and purchase the forgiveness of our sins. We would never doubt the assurance of our salvation because it was accomplished by this supreme Christ! Sadly, however, we often forget this truth. We misunderstand the person and work of Jesus.

How does verse 15 encourage you in regard to the status of your personal relationship with God?

THREE

Like I said earlier, we could sit and soak in these verses for a lifetime and never get tired or bored. But for the sake of context (and because we must keep going!), please read over the hymn in Colossians 1:15-20 again. Remember that we read this hymn in light of the whole Bible.

There are brilliant parallels for us to observe:

• Adam ("son of God," see Luke 3:38) in comparison to "the last Adam" (1 Cor. 15:45), meaning Jesus, the Son of God;

• Fallen humanity in comparison to the body of Christ (the church); and

• The first creation (which is now fallen because of our sin) in comparison to the new creation (which is being ushered in by Christ).

Adam disobeyed God, but "the last Adam" obeyed God perfectly. Adam's disobedience led to the downfall of the entire cosmos. The last Adam's obedience brings about the reconciliation of the cosmos. We discussed last week how Jesus had come to do what Adam failed to do; in particular we remembered that Jesus knew and obeyed God's will. Paul prayed that we, too, would be filled with the knowledge of God's will and be fully pleasing to God as we live in light of God's Word. This is fitting for us because we no longer belong to the kingdom of darkness, but God has transferred us to the kingdom of the Son whom He loves.

Whereas Adam and Eve were to be fruitful and multiply and serve as God's vice regents over God's first creation, in this passage Jesus is shown to be the preeminent King over the first (now fallen) creation and the new creation that is coming.

Jesus has launched the new creation by virtue of His life, death, and resurrection from the dead. Adam disobeyed God's will concerning the tree, but Jesus obeyed God's will concerning the cross/tree. Adam's downfall brought about death and destruction and spread out from the garden, but Christ's victory brings about new life and is spreading out from that garden tomb into the whole world!

Make a list of what verses 15-20 tell us about Jesus.

Let's take a closer look at how Paul has organized these verses. First, verse 15 comes before verse 16 (a brilliant observation, I might say!), and verse 16 builds on verse 15 with "For ..."

READ COLOSSIANS 1:16.

What does verse 16 encompass?

Everything in verse 16 falls under the category of the first or "old" creation that is passing away.

NOW, SKIP DOWN TO READ VERSE 18.

We'll call this the new creation.

How does Paul describe Jesus' relationship to the new creation in verse 18?

Jesus is preeminent over both the old creation and the new creation. Jesus is the heir of the old creation by His creation rights and by His rights as God's Son, just like a firstborn traditionally inherits His father's estate. Jesus is the firstborn from the dead by rights of His victory over death and resurrection from the dead. When He walked out of that garden tomb on Sunday morning, He did so as the first man in the new creation.

Jesus is the Son whom God loves, who has accomplished our redemption and the forgiveness of all our sins.

Jesus created all things and holds dominion over all things, and yet He stretched His hands out on the cross in order to offer amnesty to rebellious traitors who would cling to Him by faith.

Reflecting on what you've learned about Jesus today (or were reminded about Jesus), pray a prayer of praise to God the Father of our Lord Jesus Christ, whose Son is the radiance of His glory.

FOUR

The themes of filling and fullness come up many times in Colossians. The overall message of the letter is concerned with teaching the Colossians and us that Jesus Christ is all—if we have Christ, then we are not lacking. There is no deficiency in Him, and we do not suffer want if we are in Him. In this life we will have trouble—poverty, war, persecution, and death—yet spiritually we are already complete if we are in Christ. We are part of the new creation that will surely come in full at God's appointed time. But waiting for the day of redemption is a daily challenge (to put it lightly).

What are some of the challenges you are facing today that threaten your hope in the future God has promised to you through His Son?

In what ways are you tempted to doubt the sufficiency of Jesus Christ to meet all your needs and give you a certain hope?

Already in verses 9-10 we read Paul's prayer that we would "be *filled* with the knowledge of [God's] will in all spiritual wisdom and understanding, so as to walk in a manner worthy of the Lord, *fully* pleasing to him" (emphasis mine). In verse 19 Paul says, "For in [Christ] all the fullness of God was pleased to dwell."

A common description of Paul's Letter to the Colossians is that it is a more personalized and compact letter when compared to the letter he wrote to the church at Ephesus. Compare Colossians 1:18-19 with Ephesians 1:22-23. How does Paul describe Jesus?

Jesus cannot be described in terms that limit His sovereignty, authority, or fullness. Likewise, the church—His body—cannot be described in terms that limit her proximity to or affiliation with her Head, Jesus. He is the Head; she is His body. Christ fills His church.

God is pleased for all of His fullness to dwell in Christ. Jesus knew this—He was well aware of His deity—that He is the second person of the triune Godhead. However, many of our friends and neighbors attempt to refute this fact saying, "Jesus never claimed to be God." To this willful or otherwise ignorant denial, Jesus emphatically responds (as He did to the Jews in John 8:58), "Truly, truly, I say to you, before Abraham was, I am." How could Jesus preexist before Abraham? He is God. This is the very name of God—I AM WHO I AM—which was revealed by God in the conversation He held with Moses before the Exodus when He sent Moses to deliver the children of Israel (Ex. 3:14). Jesus identified Himself as God, which is why the Jews who heard Him say this picked up stones to try to execute Him on the spot (John 8:59).

We've traced throughout different genres of Scripture the locations of God's filling. We saw that the glory of God filled the tabernacle and later the temple. Prophets spoke about how God's glory would one day fill the entire earth. Now that Christ has ascended and poured out His Spirit on His people, the Holy Spirit now fills the church (His people). We read in Colossians 1:19 that all the fullness of God is pleased to dwell in Christ. We do not hear a hint of inadequacy or insufficiency in any description of Christ. Since Christ is fully God, He is in no way lacking.

> When we consider the scope of Paul's Letter to the Colossians, we are reminded he is describing the reasons why the believers should have confidence in Christ and not look to other things (laws, idols, traditions, etc.) for their sufficiency. How does this text—Colossians 1:19—fit into Paul's argument for Christ's sufficiency?

Now look at verse 20. What is the scope of the reconciliation Christ has accomplished?

How has Jesus accomplished this peace?

How does verse 20 fit into Paul's argument for Christ's sufficiency?

As you reflect on these verses, ask the Lord to reveal to you any areas of your life that you need to bring under submission to this truth.

Is there anything that needs to change about your priorities, perspective, or property in light of the fact of Christ's sufficiency?

The centrality of the cross cannot be overstated. It is through His shed blood at the cross that Jesus accomplished cosmic reconciliation. His work is cosmic in scope, yet immensely personal and particular. The peace that Jesus purchased for His people came at the highest possible cost—His very life. Spend some time praising God for His Son's willingness to be the sacrifice for your sin.

FIVE

Read through Colossians 1:15-23 a couple of times. In summary, these verses describe the all-powerful Christ through whom and for whom all things were created. "All things" is delineated as everything from the heavenly realm to the earthly realm and all things in between. Christ's position as head of the church is described, as is His unassailable deity: "For in him all the fullness of God was pleased to dwell" (v. 19). Through the work His Son did on the cross, God has reconciled to Himself all things.

And now the apostle turns his attention to us, the church. In light of the stunning words he uses to talk about our cosmic Christ, one might expect the apostle to use compatibly lovely depictions of us as well. But instead, we read this eye-opening line in verse 21: "And you, who once were alienated and hostile in mind, doing evil deeds."

Back in the first verses of chapter 1, Paul addresses this letter to "the saints and faithful brothers" (Col. 1:2) for whom he always thanks God (1:3). How do you reconcile these two different descriptions of the addressees?

Using the terminology of Colossians 1, describe what has happened to the Colossian believers to bring about such a radical change.

There are some corresponding references to the nature of conversion in the Letter to the Ephesians. We will look up a few of these verses from Ephesians and take notes on them. Then we'll ask and answer some questions about conversion.

READ COLOSSIANS 1:21, AND ANSWER THE FOLLOWING QUESTIONS:

Who is the willful subject of alienation from God?

Why are we willfully alienated from God?

What is the evidence of our alienation?

*NOW READ EPHESIANS 2:1-3,11-12, AND ANSWER THE
SAME QUESTIONS:*

Who is the willful subject of alienation from God?

Why are we willfully alienated from God?

What is the evidence of our alienation?

Two of the most hope-filled words a sinner could hear are these: *But God!*

> *But God, being rich in mercy, because of the great love with which
> he loved us, even when we were dead in our trespasses, made us
> alive together with Christ—by grace you have been saved.*
> **EPHESIANS 2:4-5**

Following up verse 21 in Colossians 1, we read, "he has now reconciled in his
body of flesh by his death, in order to present you holy and blameless and
above reproach before him" (v. 22).

How has God Himself solved the problem of our alienation from Him?

How did He accomplish this?

Who initiated this reconciliation?

What is the purpose of our reconciliation?

READ EPHESIANS 5:25-27.

What has Christ done, and why? For whom has He done this tremendous, cosmos-shaking act?

Paul's train of thought continues from Colossians 1:21-22 on into verse 23. There is a conditional word in this verse—a warning.

   *"**If** indeed you continue in the faith ..."*
   COLOSSIANS 1:23 (emphasis mine)

READ COLOSSIANS 1:21-23.

How are the Colossians to "continue in the faith"?

Paul uses three descriptions of the gospel in verse 23. What are they?
1. The gospel that:

2. The gospel which has:

3. The gospel of which:

The gospel has just been thrice-described. How is it possible for the Colossians to shift from the hope of this gospel?

How is it possible for you to be tempted to shift from the hope of this gospel?

Not shifting from the hope of the gospel is a continual, ongoing activity. Fidelity to the true gospel requires our utmost attention to both believing right doctrine and living consistently with the gospel. Jesus calls His disciples to "abide" in Him as He abides in us. Jesus says in John 15:

Abide in me, and I in you. As the branch cannot bear fruit by itself, unless it abides in the vine, neither can you, unless you abide in me. I am the vine; you are the branches. Whoever abides in me and I in him, he it is that bears much fruit, for apart from me you can do nothing.
JOHN 15:4-5

What is the result of abiding in Jesus as He abides in us?

Peace

What are the consequences of not abiding in Jesus?

Forfeiting Peace

Looking back over Colossians 1:15-23 and keeping in mind the whole message of Colossians, there are certainly some implications that Paul wants the believers to see and understand in regard to their irrevocable connection with the supreme and supremely-sufficient Christ.

Jude says,

> *Now to him who is able to protect you from stumbling and to make you stand in the presence of his glory, without blemish and with great joy, to the only God our Savior, through Jesus Christ our Lord, be glory, majesty, power, and authority before all time, now and forever. Amen.*
> **JUDE 24-25, CSB**

> *Personalize this benediction with your own name (e.g. "Now to him who is able to keep _____ from stumbling and to present _____ ...").*

Praise God for His Son! Praise God for the cross! As you go about the rest of your day—morning or evening—meditate on the wonder of the glorious Christ and His cross.

Take time to note below how you will apply these truths to your life.

_____

_____

_____

GROUP TIME REVIEW

Let's begin by reviewing your Personal Study from the past week.

Paul is using the strategy of teaching the believers about who Christ is in order to combat the false teaching they are facing in Colossae. How is this an effective strategy?

The ancient hymn in Colossians 1:15 and following gives us a stunning description of Jesus. One could divide the hymn into two parts. What are those two parts and what realms do they encompass?

What does it mean that Jesus is "the firstborn of all creation" (v. 15)? What does it mean that Jesus is "the firstborn from the dead" (v. 18)?

Over the course of human history, men and women have attempted different strategies to reconcile the brokenness we see all around us. Name one or two examples of these man-made attempts of reconciliation, noting their effectiveness. What has God done in order to reconcile to Himself all things? What is the effectiveness of God's reconciling work?

What are the three descriptions of the gospel Paul gives in Colossians 1:23?

WATCH VIDEO ON COLOSSIANS 1:15-23

_____
_____
_____
_____
_____
_____
_____
_____
_____
_____
_____
_____
_____
_____
_____
_____
_____
_____
_____
_____
_____
_____
_____
_____
_____
_____
_____
_____

Videos available for purchase or rent
at LifeWay.com/RaisedTogether

DISCUSS VIDEO ON COLOSSIANS 1:15-23

We all live complex, busy lives with many responsibilities and cares. How does it encourage you to know that our focus ought to be singular: the person and work of Jesus?

Discuss this statement on Colossians 1:18b from G. K. Beale's New Testament Biblical Theology: "Christ is the theological-geographical point from which the rest of the new creation spreads."[1]

How many mediators between God and man have you come across in your life? What is their plan for reconciliation?

How is Jesus Christ "God's solution to the cosmic defiance of His creatures"?

What are some safeguards that can help prevent a person from shifting from the hope of the gospel?

CLOSE

Jesus Christ alone is worthy of our worship. He alone is supreme by means of His creation and re-creation rights over all things. He alone is sufficient to be the one mediator between God and man. Is there anyone present today who is uncertain if she is reconciled to God through His Son? Please do not leave today's meeting without sitting down with a discussion leader or a friend to talk about this eternally significant matter. Pray together that God would create new life in anyone among you who is not yet raised together with Christ. Pray that God would use you to be a messenger of His reconciling work on the cross.

1. G. K. Beale, *A New Testament Biblical Theology: The Unfolding of the Old Testament in the New* (Grand Rapids: Baker Academic, 2011), 544.

SESSION 4:
COLOSSIANS 1:24–2:5

ONE

Welcome to your Personal Study of Colossians 1:24–2:5. When someone asks you, "What is it that you do?" there are many ways to respond. You could discuss your schedule in detail and name all of the tasks you are responsible to carry out. You could choose to answer with a general description of your work: "I look after the accounting for such-and-such company," or "I raise our children, and I sell this-or-that thing." When you're answering the "so, what is it that you do" question, you also could just give one of your roles in the form of a title: "physician's assistant" or "translator" or "homemaker" or fill-in-the-blank.

As Paul describes his ministry in this passage he comes at it from many angles—he tells us his tasks, his title, his goals, and his motive. Today we are going to look at the overview of our passage this week—Colossians 1:24–2:5—and scratch the surface with some general questions. Later on in the week we will dig deeper into some of the terms and phrases Paul uses here. But before we get started, let's pray for God's help in our study of His Word.

> Father, thank You for causing the sun to rise on me today. Through Your Son You created all things—things in heaven and things on earth. All things are created through Him and for Him. When I consider Your power to create everything and give life to whom You will, I am in awe that You would care for me, a sinner who deserves Your wrath. Father, thank You for sending Jesus to die for my sin on the cross. Thank You for fulfilling Your promise to Adam to send a serpent-crusher, Your promise to Abraham to bring about worldwide blessing through him, Your promise to David that his

heir would sit on the throne forever, and Your promise to Jesus to give Him the nations for His inheritance. Would Your Spirit help me to understand Your Word as I read it, seek to understand it, and apply it to my life today? I want to live by Your Word, for it is my very life. In Jesus' name I pray, Amen.

READ THROUGH COLOSSIANS 1:24–2:5 SEVERAL TIMES.

What are some of the key words or phrases Paul uses to tell us about his ministry?

Summarize Paul's ministry in one sentence.

(Challenge!) Summarize Paul's ministry in one word.

What is Paul's message?

What is Paul's goal in proclaiming this message?

Considering the context of this letter, why does Paul have a "warning" (v. 28) aspect to his ministry?

TWO

Today we are going to zoom in on the first verse in our passage, Colossians 1:24: "Now I rejoice in my sufferings for your sake, and in my flesh I am filling up what is lacking in Christ's afflictions for the sake of his body, that is, the church."

This verse can be misconstrued to say that the work Jesus did on the cross was not enough to save us, but the term "Christ's afflictions" does not have the atonement in view. "Christ's afflictions" encompasses all the Messiah endured in His earthly ministry and continues to endure in His ongoing ministry by His Spirit while His body here on earth is maligned, beaten, beheaded, whipped, marginalized, and otherwise persecuted for century after bloody century. However, there are some who misconstrue the term "Christ's afflictions" to surmise that what Jesus suffered on the cross cannot fully expiate our sin. They say that we, therefore, must now supplement the work of Jesus and earn merit in our own suffering and only then we can be presented blameless before God.

How does Paul refute this false teaching? (Hint: Look back in Colossians 1:22.)

What do you think is the root of the issue in this false teaching? Why would people be willing to embrace a teaching that says they must add to Christ's work on the cross?

Jesus never lost the joy of His ministry. Isaiah 53 gives us a vivid description of the suffering the Messiah would endure for His people. Jesus knew all of this was ahead of Him as He went to the cross.

READ ISAIAH 53, AND MAKE NOTES BELOW OF KEY PHRASES THAT STAND OUT TO YOU.

Even as Jesus suffered for our sake and endured the cross, He was fixed on the joy that was set before Him. Hebrews 12:2 says,

> *Looking to Jesus, the founder and perfecter of our faith, **who for the joy that was set before him endured the cross, despising the shame,** and is seated at the right hand of the throne of God.*
> **HEBREWS 12:2 (emphasis mine)**

So with joy Jesus suffered for Paul to save Paul, and now in Colossians 1:24, Paul is suffering for the sake of Christ's body and he does so with joy. Because the world can no longer persecute Jesus who has now ascended back into heaven, the world turns its attention to persecute Jesus' body, the church.

When Jesus knocked Saul the persecutor of the church off his horse in Acts, He called him to be Paul the apostle to the Gentiles (temporarily blinding him in the process). When a disciple named Ananias was told in a vision to go lay hands on Saul so he would regain his sight and was hesitant to embrace Paul, Jesus assured Ananias,

> *Go, for he is a chosen instrument of mine to carry my name before the Gentiles and kings and the children of Israel. For I will show him how much he must suffer for the sake of my name.*
> **ACTS 9:15-16**

This call to apostleship and suffering was not a punishment for Paul from Christ, as though Paul must now do penance for his former persecution of the church. Not at all. This call to ministry (and every call to ministry) is an invitation to fellowship.

While Paul sat in a Roman jail (for the sake of Christ; see Phil. 1:13), he talked about this particular fellowship with Christ, saying it is his goal. Read Philippians 3:10. What does Paul want to know?

In several places in his letters Paul describes the terrible sufferings he endures for the sake of the church, and near the end of his ministry his conclusion concerning his many trials is this:

> **Therefore I endure everything for the sake of the elect, that they also may obtain the salvation that is in Christ Jesus with eternal glory.**
> **2 TIMOTHY 2:10**

Keeping in mind the passage we are studying in Colossians, what do you think Paul means that his suffering is for the sake of the elect?

Consider the godly men and women in your life. In what ways are they suffering while they wait for the day of redemption? What is the outcome of their joyful suffering in your life?

Life is full of pain because we live in a fallen world. And when we are joined to Christ, the One whom the world hates most, we will assuredly endure suffering. Take a few moments to reflect on whatever suffering and tribulation you are facing during this season, and ask God to give you unshakable joy and an eternal perspective.

THREE

We've seen that Paul's ministry is full of tremendous pain, and yet it is also joy-filled. Who would choose such a career? Look back to his greeting in Colossians 1:1.

How did Paul's ministry come about?

How does Paul further clarify his ministry in Colossians 1:25?

A steward is not an owner, but rather, one who manages something on behalf of an owner. God was not in any way obligated to make Paul a steward of His grace and send him to the Gentiles, so Paul sees the stewardship of his ministry as an immense, undeserved privilege.

In Colossians 1:25-29, Paul further describes his ministry. What are the parameters of his ministry? What is his mission?

Who gave Paul this mission?

Why did God send Paul to the Gentiles?

How does Paul describe to King Agrippa his calling into ministry in Acts 26:1-23?

Look back to the first Personal Study of this week. Read your summary of Paul's message.

Why is it significant that God would send Paul to the Gentiles to proclaim this message?

READ 2 CORINTHIANS 4:5.

Paul does not exercise a harsh, authoritarian leadership among the churches, but he consistently appeals to them as their "servant" or "minister." Paul never proclaims himself, but Christ alone.

Why has Paul reminded the Colossians of his calling and apostleship in this letter?

How does Paul's example of serving others while enduring suffering motivate you?

READ 1 PETER 4:10.

How are you using the gifts God has given you to serve others?

What are some ways you could be a better steward of these gifts?

Paul is clear in giving credit for his ministry to Jesus Himself. Jesus called him to ministry, Jesus gives him joy in ministry, and Jesus gives him the strength he needs to serve, "struggling with all his energy that he powerfully works within me" (Col. 1:29).

How has God called you to serve Him? Where has He sovereignly placed you in ministry? Are you careful to proclaim Christ, making His gospel central to your service among others? Spend some time reflecting on these questions today, and use the space below to write down your thoughts and ideas.

FOUR

Paul's description of his ministry and his heart for the people he serves has come at a strategic moment in this letter. He doesn't want the people he loves to be deluded with plausible arguments and led astray from Christ.

> *READ THROUGH COLOSSIANS 2:1-5 SEVERAL TIMES. The apostle is sharing his heart, showing the Colossians (and others) how much he cares for them.*

> *What is the "struggle" (v. 1) that Paul refers to? Why is it important that his readers know about his great struggle?*

> *Who is the object of Paul's concern? Look up the location of this city on a map in your Bible or online.*

> *There are other believers who would have received Paul's Letter to the Colossians. Who does Paul mention in Colossians 4:15-17?*

Paul's desire for the believers is "that their hearts may be encouraged, being knit together in love, to reach all the riches of full assurance of understanding and the knowledge of God's mystery, which is Christ" (Col. 2:2). In keeping with the theme of "fullness" in his letter, he identifies yet another aspect of the Christian life that they may have: full assurance of understanding.

> *What are the riches associated with assurance? Name the benefits one may experience when they have full assurance of something.*

What kind of assurance does Paul desire his readers to have? To what degree or measure does he want them to have this assurance?

The knowledge of God's mystery is Christ—namely, God's plan of salvation through Christ. Do you have full assurance of understanding of the gospel?

Hebrews 11:1 succinctly describes the nature of faith:

Now faith is the assurance of things hoped for, the conviction of things not seen.
HEBREWS 11:1

Faith is not a gamble or a guess; it is assurance. In some cultures assurance is believed to be evidence of arrogant character. In other cultures, someone who is confident and "sure of herself" is admired. Biblically-speaking, we hope that we may "reach all the riches of full assurance of understanding and the knowledge of God's mystery, which is Christ" (Col. 2:2).

What is your personal reaction to Paul's hope for his readers to have full assurance? Do you believe it is possible to reach this kind of full assurance? Why or why not?

What words would you use to describe your faith in Christ? Would you describe your belief in Jesus as firm like the apostle describes the faith of the Colossians (v. 5)? Explain.

FIVE

Paul has been rehearsing his call to ministry and his desire for the Colossians to embrace his teaching concerning Christ and the Christian life.

As a summary for this section of his letter, Paul says,

> *I say this in order that no one may delude you with plausible*
> *arguments.*
> **COLOSSIANS 2:4**

What follows in the rest of the letter are itemized plausible arguments by which the believers are in danger of being deluded. His concern for them is heightened, because he is not physically there with the church. Nonetheless, he is "rejoicing to see your good order and the firmness of your faith in Christ" (Col. 2:5).

During this Personal Study, we will look back over what we've read in Colossians up to this point. It is important for us to do so, because in the very next verse (spoiler alert!), Paul is going to begin to lay out an incredible series of applications for us to follow so that our lives will be in line with what he has already taught. These applications stand in contrast to the deluding, plausible arguments that Paul will dismantle, demonstrating their lack of credibility.

We'll go backward in the text, starting with what we've most recently read, namely Paul's ministry calling, qualifications, and heart.

READ COLOSSIANS 1:24–2:5, AND COMPLETE THE SUMMARY STATEMENTS:

Paul became a minister of the church according to:

Paul's stewardship from God is to make the word of God:

The mystery hidden for ages was:

Paul proclaims Christ, warning and teaching everyone with all wisdom, so that:

In order to present everyone mature in Christ, the Christ who must be proclaimed is the One proclaimed by Paul and the other apostles. A different message would not be the gospel at all, and would only be effective for our condemnation. Colossians 1:15-23 contains a breathtaking description of Jesus and the effects of His work that reconciles us to God.

Write down some key phrases from Colossians 1:15-23 concerning the person of Jesus Christ.

Now write down phrases from the text that describe His work on the cross and its effect on the cosmos (which includes everything you can see and can't see).

Following the logic of Paul's presentation of the good news and his authority as an apostle, one is led to wonder how they can be fully assured that what they are believing is the word of truth. The answer, of course, is that we need to know God's Word, the Bible! How can we understand God's mystery (God's plan of salvation through Christ) if we do not know God's Word? At this point in our study in Colossians we can clearly see Paul's strategy in strengthening the believers at Colossae: proclaim Christ and the plausible arguments against Christ will be exposed as the demonic lies that they are.

MOVING BACKWARD IN THE TEXT STILL, WE REVISIT COLOSSIANS 1:1-14, WHICH OUTLINES PAUL'S PRAYER REQUESTS FOR THE YOUNG CHURCH IN THE LYCUS VALLEY. READ COLOSSIANS 1:1-14.

Why is Paul thankful for the report he has heard from Epaphras about the Colossians?

Briefly summarize what he is praying for them.

As the rest of Colossians unfolds and we read the radical, new creation ethic Paul is teaching, we will see how his prayer requests directly connect to the results he has in mind via his teaching. The Christian life Paul describes, exhorts, and commands in the chapters that follow flow right out of these prayer requests and dismantle the demonic doctrines that were threatening the church plant.

Who is Paul's teaching for? How much wisdom does it involve? The answers are in Colossians 1:28.

What is the danger in teaching only some of the people in the church and not all of them? What is the danger of only teaching some of the counsel of God and not all of it?

In order to reach maturity in Christ—as far as we are able in this *eschaton* before Christ returns—we must know and obey God's Word. We must know Christ and everything He is and everything He does in and through us. Christian maturity is Paul's goal for all believers everywhere; there are no second-rate Christians in the family of God.

Describe your own goals in knowing God more and more. How are you going about those goals?

What are some ways you would like to mature and grow in your faith?

GROUP TIME REVIEW

Let's begin by reviewing your Personal Study from the past week.

Summarize Paul's ministry in one sentence. What one word does Paul use to summarize his message?

Why does Paul have a warning and admonishing aspect to his ministry?

What does it mean that Paul's suffering is filling up what is lacking in Christ's afflictions? What does the term "lacking" mean?

How did hearing Paul's description of his ministry impact you? What thoughts did it give you about your own ministry?

What words would you use to describe your faith in Christ?

WATCH VIDEO ON COLOSSIANS 1:24–2:5

Videos available for purchase or rent
at LifeWay.com/RaisedTogether

DISCUSS VIDEO ON COLOSSIANS 1:24–2:5

How are you doing in the areas of teaching and correcting as you serve one another in the body of Christ? Are you taking advantage of opportunities to be taught and edified by others? How has God equipped you to serve others in these ways?

Perhaps you are not in vocational ministry, but have you considered that if you are a believer, then He has made you to be a priest in a priesthood (i.e., the church; see 1 Pet. 2:5,9)? How does your role as a priest unto God inform the way you view your church membership, home life, career, schedule, and errands?

What has been your experience in suffering as you serve the Lord? And how has your joy in ministry been sustained?

How can we pray for one another's ministries this week?

_____

_____

_____

_____

_____

_____

_____

_____

_____

CLOSE

We may not have been called to ministry in the same way as Paul (i.e., knocked to the ground and blinded) or to the same degree as Paul (i.e., apostle to the Gentiles), but if we are in Christ, then we are called to serve Him. Christ reconciled us to God on the cross, and He has given us the ministry of reconciliation. Read 2 Corinthians 5:17-21 together. Pray for one another to have joy even as you suffer for Christ and lift up any prayer requests you have concerning the various ministries in which you are serving (e.g., your church, your home, your work, etc.).

SESSION 5:

COLOSSIANS
2:6-23

ONE

Welcome back! The rest of Colossians 2 marks a transition of sorts for the apostle Paul, in which he directs his energies toward explicit exhortation in light of the doctrine he has already laid out in previous verses. And it isn't as though he is going to stop teaching, either! Not at all. Paul will continue to admonish and strengthen the believers' faith through teaching them rich doctrine. As we've seen over and over again throughout this letter, Paul's strategy in encouraging this young church toward maturity is to impart truth and refute error through teaching them doctrine.

So often we are not patient enough to do the work of intensely studying doctrine. It's human nature to prefer quick fixes, life "hacks," and "five steps to solve the issue at hand." How do you see this propensity at work in your own life?

What are your expectations of Colossians 2 in light of the "heads-up" that there is more rich doctrine to apply?

Let's pray for God's help to understand and apply His Word to our lives.

Father, we come to You as needy and fragile as ever. It is Your power that both holds our lives together and keeps the planets and stars in their places. How desperately we need You! The cares and worries of our hearts are many today, but Your Word revives our souls. Would Your Spirit help clear away any distractions as we seek to read, examine, and obey Your Word in Colossians 2. Help us to see the beauty of Your Son and give us the grace we need to worship Him with everything we have and everything we are. In Jesus' name we pray, Amen.

Let's start today's Personal Study by reading over Colossians 2:6-23 several times slowly. Use the space below to write down the key words that stand out to you in this text.

The term "therefore" appears in this text twice (vv. 6,16). A commonly used question to ask of a passage whenever you see the term "therefore" is to ask "What is this there for?"

As you read over Colossians 2:6-23, what did you notice about Paul's presentation of his exhortation to the young converts? How did he organize his teaching? What are the "therefores" there for?

Several references to the Old Testament appear in this passage. Some of them are explicitly mentioned and others he alludes to indirectly. All of these mentions—direct or indirect—are profoundly intentional and useful for our edification. Let's start to look more closely.

What references to Old Testament worship did you notice?

Why do you suppose Paul is bringing them into this discussion of the sufficiency and supremacy of Jesus Christ?

In addition to references to Old Testament practices, Paul continues weaving several Colossian themes throughout chapter 2. What issues does he bring up in chapter 2 that he has already raised in chapter 1?

NOW LET'S READ VERSES 6-7, PAUL'S INTRODUCTORY REMARKS FOR THIS SECTION OF EXHORTATION.

What assumptions does Paul say he is making concerning who his readers are and what has happened to them?

Friend, could Paul make these same assumptions about you? If so, what is the apostle's exhortation to you? If not, what do you suppose Paul might say to encourage you today?

Paul employs two different metaphors in these two verses—a plant and a building. Referring back to the doctrine Paul has already taught and referred to in the previous chapter, in what way does a church resemble a rooted plant? In what way does a church resemble an established building?

What is "the faith" the Colossians have been taught? (Hint: Again, refer back to chapter 1.)

TWO

I think Colossians 2:6-7 could serve as a microcosm of this entire letter. The Christ Jesus whom Paul has preached is the Lord. The Colossians have received this cosmic Christ, and so now, naturally, they are to live in light of their allegiance to Him. They are to remain "in Christ" with overflowing thankfulness as a distinguishing mark of their fundamental transformation and growth.

Now in verse 8 and following, the apostle turns his attention to specific false teachings that could lead the new believers to walk a different way, tear up their roots, and shake the foundations of their established faith.

FIRST, READ COLOSSIANS 1:15-20, AND THEN READ 2:8-10.

What are the things Paul lists in verse 8 that may take the young believers captive?

What (Who!) does Paul state is the opposite of these hostile things?

What argument does Paul give in verses 9-10 to persuade his readers to avoid being taken captive by the hostile things mentioned in verse 8?

The words "rule and authority" in verse 10 refer to angelic beings (both good and evil; see also Eph.1:21-23).

SKIP DOWN AND READ COLOSSIANS 2:14-15.

What has happened to the evil "rulers and authorities" (v. 15)?

How did this happen?

With this knowledge in mind, why is it important for the Colossians to recall both that Christ is the Head, even of all rule and authority, and that these invisible powers have been disarmed and shamed in front of the entire watching cosmos? (Hint: Look at Paul's admonition in v. 18.)

Often when we think of the cross we rightly recall that this is the place where our sins were forgiven and atoned for by the blood of Jesus. Perhaps less often, we recall that the cross is the place where the head of the serpent—God's enemy— was crushed (see Gen. 3:15). These two things (the forgiveness of our sins and the defeat of God's enemy) happened at the cross of Jesus Christ. But how often do we remember and appreciate that several other things happened that weekend over two thousand years ago?

> *You were also circumcised in him with a circumcision not done with hands, by putting off the body of flesh, in the circumcision of Christ, when you were buried with him in baptism, in which you were also raised with him through faith in the working of God, who raised him from the dead. And when you were dead in trespasses and in the uncircumcision of your flesh, he made you alive with him and forgave us all our trespasses. He erased the certificate of debt, with its obligations, that was against us and opposed to us, and has taken it away by nailing it to the cross.*
> **COLOSSIANS 2:11-14, CSB**

Believer, as Paul explains what happened to Christ on the cross and in His resurrection from the dead, he wants you to see what happened to you as well.

According to these verses, what happened to Christ?

What happened to believers in Christ?

We're going to begin to write down some of the implications for this rich doctrine. Clearly, Paul wants our primary application to be worshiping the supreme and all-sufficient Christ to whom all glory and honor are due.

What are some of the personal applications of this text? Ask God to show you any areas of your life—perspectives, beliefs, assumptions, or otherwise—that are not according to Christ.

As specific things come to your mind, ask the Lord to forgive you for trusting in those things. Ask for His Spirit's help to live in light of the fact that you have been raised together with Jesus. If you are not a believer, ask the Lord to reveal Himself to you in His Word and to show you who you are—whether you are yet raised with Him from the dead.

THREE

Dear friend, welcome to a day of talking about circumcision. You may need an extra cup of coffee for this one. Now, I realize that the practice of circumcision may not come to your mind on a regular basis (unless, perhaps, you are a pediatrician or a urologist!). However, in the Old Testament the subject of circumcision was of everyday concern according to the Jewish Law. It was the primary physical mark of God's people in those days and was necessary for their acceptable worship unto God. So, why has Paul brought up the topic of circumcision to a church plant of Gentile believers?

We know from our overview and summarizing themes of this letter that the false teaching Paul is addressing concerns attacks on the sufficiency and supremacy of Jesus Christ. Therefore, it is safe to assume that any and every thing Paul contrasts here as contrary to Christ is insufficient for our salvation and growth in godliness. On the list of things that are insufficient: physical circumcision. Circumcision of the foreskin is not enough for salvation—it never was. Paul explains this elsewhere in Romans 2:

> *For no one is a Jew who is merely one outwardly, nor is circumcision outward and physical. But a Jew is one inwardly, and circumcision is a matter of the heart, by the Spirit, not by the letter. His praise is not from man but from God.*
> **ROMANS 2:28-29**

God's prophets repeatedly reminded Israel that this tiny cut into the foreskin was a picture of something that was far more than skin deep.

> *Read the following passages from the Old Testament concerning circumcision, summarizing them as you read:*
>
> *Deuteronomy 10:16*

Deuteronomy 30:6

Jeremiah 4:4

Jeremiah 9:25-26

Ezekiel 44:7

TURN BACK TO COLOSSIANS 2:11-14.

What is the result of the circumcision "made without hands" (v. 11), which has happened to believers in Christ?

Since Jesus has made "foreigners, uncircumcised in heart and flesh" (Ezek. 44:7) acceptable to God, what does that mean regarding any spiritual benefit of physical circumcision?

How would this have strengthened the faith of the Colossians who were being taken captive by false teaching concerning Jewish doctrine?

Through highlighting that physical circumcision is our act of removing (with hands) a very tiny piece of flesh and spiritual circumcision is God's act of removing (without hands) the sinful flesh itself, we see the total supremacy of Christ for our salvation. We see the sufficiency of Christ in comparison to the preparatory role of the worship prescribed in the Jewish temple.

How does Paul's teaching concerning the supremacy of Christ's work over physical circumcision strengthen your faith today?

PAUL ALSO MENTIONS BAPTISM IN COLOSSIANS 2:

Having been buried with him in baptism, in which you were also raised with him through faith in the powerful working of God, who raised him from the dead.
COLOSSIANS 2:12

What does Paul teach here concerning what happened to us (believers in Christ) on that weekend two thousand years ago?

If we are in Christ, then we are now so closely associated with Him that we are to regard ourselves as having been crucified with Him, buried with Him in the grave, and raised with Him from the dead. There's no paper record of our sin debt involved in verse 14. The sin that bore record against us in God's courtroom was placed on Christ as He bore our sin in His body (see Rom. 8:3; 2 Cor. 5:21; Gal. 3:13). Jesus was physically nailed to the cross. And there's no water involved in verse 12. Paul is referring to the garden tomb. Once again we see a tremendous gospel truth of our new identity of having been taken out of the first Adam and placed in "the last Adam," Jesus Christ. As Paul says elsewhere in 1 Corinthians,

> For as in Adam all die, so also in Christ shall all be made alive.
> **1 CORINTHIANS 15:22**

Praise the Lord!

Believing friend, spend some time reflecting on your salvation in Christ by meditating on the pictures Paul gives us here in Colossians 2:11-15. Abounding in thanksgiving, write down your reflections or a prayer in the space below.

To my friends who are not yet believers, would you pray that God would soften your heart? Deuteronomy 10:16 says, "Circumcise therefore the foreskin of your heart, and be no longer stubborn." Only Jesus Christ crucified for your sins and raised for your justification can save you. I am praying that the Spirit would work in your heart today.

FOUR

In Colossians 2:6-23 we have three warning statements from Paul. There is a general, overall warning (v. 8), followed by specific warnings in verses 16 and 18.

Summarize the warnings in the space below.

Colossians 2:8 — Don't let anyone _____ you.

Colossians 2:16 — Don't let anyone _____ you.

Colossians 2:18 — Don't let anyone _____ you.

Paul is continuing his strategy of building up the believers in the truth while he addresses the false teaching that has crept into their church.

What is the reason Paul gives for his warnings in this text?

Now, we must be clear at this point that Paul is not teaching the Colossians that they are sinless, and that is why they shouldn't let others condemn or disqualify them. For clarification on this subject we can look at 1 John 1:8-10, which summarizes the perspective believers ought to have regarding their sin.

If we say we have no sin, we deceive ourselves, and the truth is not in us. If we confess our sins, he is faithful and just to forgive us our sins and to cleanse us from all unrighteousness. If we say we have not sinned, we make him a liar, and his word is not in us.
1 JOHN 1:8-10

Does your attitude toward your sin reflect this truth? How are you challenged to live in light of these truths?

Perhaps (or perhaps not) the things listed in verses 16-18 may seem foreign to you. In all of our various contexts around the world, the Christian church is faced with various challenges to the steadfastness of our faith in Christ alone for salvation. The false teaching that a woman is faced with while riding the elevator up a high-rise in Sendai may look very different to the false teaching that a sister grapples with as she sits on a lakeside bench in Nakhchivan.

> *Based on what you have learned so far in your study of Colossians, what is at the root of all false teaching?*

> *Do you face false teaching in your particular context? What is it?*

> *How does the word of truth you have received from Paul's teaching address that false teaching?*

We are not unlike the Colossian believers who had a case of spiritual FOMO (fear of missing out). In general, we feel insecure about our spirituality, not because we think that Christ is lacking in some way, but because we look to the right or to the left at others and compare ourselves to them. In Jeremiah 23:23-32 we read about false prophets who incite this kind of dissatisfaction with God's Word for a living.

> *READ JEREMIAH 23:23-32.*

> *What do the false teachers of Colossae have in common with the false prophets in this passage?*

Paul cuts off the lifeblood of our spiritual FOMO by exalting Christ—over and over again. Paul emphasizes that we do not need to look to the false teachers in order to see what they have or to seek their approval.

READ COLOSSIANS 2:19.

What does it mean to live "holding fast to the Head"?

What happens when we hold fast to the Head?

How about you, friend? How is your growth in Christ? What kind of soil are you growing in? Are you growing in the fertile soil of Christian community in a local church, being fed by nourishing, expository sermons and Bible study week in and week out? Reflect on these questions in the space below.

FIVE

We're nearly at the end of our longest portion of study in Colossians. To refresh your memory, read the entire letter of Colossians quickly through. Then read Colossians 2:20-23 two or three times through again. The false teachers at Colossae were essentially denying that the "substance belongs to Christ" (v. 17). Today we're going to examine how Paul picks apart this horrific denial of the supremacy and sufficiency of Christ and exhorts us to hold fast to the Head, Christ Himself.

In verse 20, Paul mentions our death. It is a particular death he has already mentioned in previous verses. Theologian G. K. Beale explains the meaning of "elemental spirits of the world" in verse 20:

> The most usual meaning of *stoicheia* in the Greek world, however, is the four basic elements of the cosmos: air, fire, water, and earth. (As illustrated in e.g., 2 Pet. 3:10, though here the "elements" of cosmos are destroyed by means of fire.) How could this basic meaning have relevance for Colossians 2? The old, fallen cosmic order was based on cosmic "elements." These elements included moral or spiritual "elements of division among humanity," ultimately held in place by the devil and his evil forces.[1]

Describe the death Paul is talking about in verse 20.

In addition to referring explicitly to our death with Christ, Paul mentions something about our life. He states it negatively "as if you were still alive in the world," meaning that we are not still alive in the world.

What do you think Paul means by this statement? How are we not still alive in the world?

The regulations mentioned in verse 21 are likely specific rules that the false teachers were attempting to enforce (versus suggest or recommend voluntarily) in Colossae. The promise made was that it would be life-giving to the Colossian believers to submit to these regulations.

What argument does Paul give against this false promise?

Jesus confronted religious leaders many times during His earthly ministry precisely on the grounds of their man-made traditions.

READ MARK 7:5-9.

What reason does Jesus give for rejecting the traditions of the religious men?

Paul has sufficiently warned us against submitting ourselves to such rules because of their deceptive promises and damning consequences. And in order to be duly warned, we need to understand why these distractions are so tempting for us.

Name an example of "self-made religion" (Col. 2:23). How does such self-made religion have an appearance of wisdom?

Name an example of "asceticism and severity to the body." How does "asceticism and severity to the body" have an appearance of wisdom?

Self-made religion, asceticism, and severity to the body can only over-promise and under-deliver. What is the deceptive promise these things make?

How does Paul refute their deceptive promise (see vv. 22-23)?

It may seem odd to reflect on how things perish as they are used, but it would do us good to remember this on occasion. What are the things that physically, biologically, chemically, or otherwise happen to earthly things that we handle, taste, and touch?

What is the obvious difference between these perishable things and Christ?

"Do not handle, Do not taste, Do not touch" (v. 21) is a common refrain in religious communities all over the world. Can you think of such a rule? What are some things that would be unthinkable for you to eat? Or unthinkable for your neighbor to have in their home? Essentially, we all do this. Even those who do not self-identify as "religious" subject themselves to these religious rules and keep them religiously. It is ironic that there are communities of people would outright deny that religion is the reason for their rules. To test this theory, simply ask a friend to give you the reason for their rule. "Why don't you ever eat this or that?" "Why do you always buy from this or that company?" At the base of their reasoning is a religiously-held (or overtly religious) belief—beliefs about the nature and purpose of humanity and the world, including a moral code to follow.

Today's Personal Study shows the sobering reality of living in the shadows. Life in the shadows, clinging to perishable things, is not really life at all. We need to hold fast to the Head—to Christ—to whom the substance belongs. Let's not be satisfied with the shadowy things; let's spur one another on to cling to Christ. Only the gospel frees us from living for the divisive elements of this world and from slavery to our sin.

The world has been crucified to us and we have been crucified to the world. Neither circumcision is anything, nor uncircumcision, but a new creation. If we are in Christ, then we live in the inaugurated new creation—indeed, we are part of the new creation. We've stepped out of the shadows and into the light of Christ.

1. G. K. Beale, *A New Testament Biblical Theology: The Unfolding of the Old Testament in the New* (Grand Rapids: Baker Academic, 2011), 874.

GROUP TIME REVIEW

Let's begin by reviewing your Personal Study from the past week.

What were your expectations of Colossians 2 in light of the "heads-up" that there was more rich doctrine to apply?

What is "the faith" the Colossians have been taught? (Hint: Again, refer back to Session 1.)

If someone would bravely share a recap of Paul's teaching concerning circumcision, others may answer this question: How does Paul's teaching concerning the supremacy of Christ's work over physical circumcision strengthen your faith today?

Based on what you have learned so far in your study of Colossians, what is at the root of all false teaching?

What is so deceptive about man-made regulations? What is the obvious difference between these rules and perishable things and the living Christ?

WATCH VIDEO ON COLOSSIANS 2:6-23

Videos available for purchase or rent at LifeWay.com/RaisedTogether

DISCUSS VIDEO ON COLOSSIANS 2:6-23

How would you explain to someone the meaning of the phrase "the substance belongs to Christ" (v. 17)?

What are some of the ways you are tempted to feel insecure concerning your spirituality?

How does the doctrine of union with Jesus encourage you?

_____

_____

_____

_____

_____

_____

_____

_____

_____

_____

_____

_____

_____

_____

_____

_____

CLOSE

This is an intensely personal passage. It hits us at the core of our beings to entertain thoughts of insecurity about our completeness or fullness spiritually-speaking. And it hits us on a very practical level as we might be a little unsure about following "the rules"—all the do not handle, taste, or touch regulations in our societies. How can you encourage one another in this regard? Split up into small groups or pairs to debrief this passage with each other and discuss how God's Word directly addresses the things you are facing today. Pray for one another in closing.

SESSION 6:

COLOSSIANS
3:1-11

ONE

Welcome back! We are now diving deep into the new creational ethic Paul teaches in Colossians. We're getting into the nitty-gritty details of what it looks like for our lives to line up with the facts of Christ's death on our behalf, His resurrection from the dead in power, His ascension to the right hand of God, and His imminent return in glory.

Let's pray for God's help as we open up His Word today:

> Father, thank You for yet another day when we have experienced Your patience and mercy. Thank You that You never change, though the world around us is in constant turmoil. Steady our hearts and minds on Christ through Your Word. Show us what it means to live in light of who You have made us to be in Your Son. Thrill our hearts with Your love. Show us our sin. Give us boldness to repent and cling to Christ. And assure us of Your forgiveness through Your Spirit. In Jesus' name we pray, Amen.

READ THROUGH COLOSSIANS 3:1-11 THREE TIMES, AND THEN RE-READ THE ENTIRE LETTER TO THE COLOSSIANS.

In view of the entire Letter to the Colossians, what is the context for this passage (3:1-11)?

What motive does Paul give to the Colossians for following his instructions?

Not carnality but Christ "all is Christ"

LET'S LOOK CLOSELY AT VERSES 1-4 FOR TODAY'S PERSONAL STUDY.

Once again, the apostle is talking about life and death. Following his teaching on circumcision and baptism, now we read about resurrection, ascension, and glorification. Paul wants his readers to see how intimately they are connected to Christ now that they are in Him. His instructions to Christians are the direct result of their new identity in Christ.

According to verse 1, who are the two persons who have been raised?

READ ACTS 1:1-11, WHICH RECORDS WHAT HAPPENED WHEN CHRIST ASCENDED AND THE EVENTS THAT IMMEDIATELY FOLLOWED.

What occurred in this passage?

Read the following passages regarding where Christ is now, making note of its location in the spaces below:

Ephesians 1:20

Hebrews 8:1

Right hand of the Father

Hebrews 12:2

Revelation 5:1

pleading our case

READ MARK 14:62.

Where did Jesus tell people He would be after He accomplished the work He came to do on the cross?

You probably noticed in Colossians 3:1-4 that one day Christ is going to return from the throne in heaven in order to do something else.

What is the manner in which He will return, and why?

In the clouds... rapture

Who will appear with Christ on that day and in what condition will they be in?

The first things Paul points out about what is consistent with our new creation life is that which involves our desires and our minds. Think of something you want. (Anything!) When you are seeking something, what are you doing?

How involved are your time, energy, money, and thoughts when you are seeking after something?

• Prayer & fasting

What does it look like for you to set your mind on something?

lifestyle/culture

What is the reason Paul gives for these explicit commands to "seek" (v. 1) and "set your minds" (v. 2)?

One implication of Colossians 3:1-4 is that both Christ and His bride, the church, are not yet revealed to the world in glory. At this moment in time, it appears to the world as though Christ and His people are defeated, though this is not the case in reality.

What assurances do you personally receive through this passage?

Verse 2 is challenging! What are "things that are above"? (Hint: Who is above?) How are you challenged by this verse?

TWO

In our first Personal Study this week, we saw several different realities occurring at the same time. In Colossians 3:1-4, Paul teaches that we "have died" and "been raised with Christ." Our lives are "hidden with Christ in God." And something is going to happen to us.

> *When Christ who is your life appears, then you also will appear with him in glory.*
> **COLOSSIANS 3:4**

To that end, we are to live in congruence with those realities—that of our death and resurrection with Christ. We are to seek and set our minds on the things that are above. This is the life that is consistent with our being made to be part of God's new creation.

It is interesting to note the connection Jesus makes between our calling to constantly seek God's kingdom and our anxiety about the things here on the earth. In His Sermon on the Mount recorded in Matthew 5–7, Jesus teaches us what life in His kingdom is like.

READ MATTHEW 6:25-34.

What connections do you see between Jesus' teaching in this passage and our current passage in Colossians 3?

NOW LOOK A FEW VERSES DOWN TO READ MATTHEW 7:7-11.

What does Jesus teach us about His Father's willingness to answer us when we are seeking things that are above?

NOW LOOK A FEW MORE VERSES DOWN TO MATTHEW 7:15-20.

Jesus warns people about false teachers who will seek to lead them astray. Paul also warns us about false teachers here in Colossians.

What are the commonalities between the false teachers whom Jesus describes and the false teachers whom Paul describes?

Assimilating what you have learned so far in Colossians, what is the nature of "true worship"?

What is true worship based on?

Who mediates this worship, and how?

In what ways are you tempted to feel insecure about your relationship with God?

How does the knowledge of God the Father's seeking you out alleviate your anxiety?

If your heavenly Father has lovingly provided everything you need in order to be right with Him (see John 3:16), what use are the things on earth?

Now, it is important to recall that Paul is not advocating a harshly ascetic lifestyle, such as the one he criticizes in chapter 2!

If the apostle is neither advocating asceticism nor renouncing God's good gifts, what is the aim of his exhortation in Colossians 3:2?

How can you practically tell if you are seeking the things that are above?

What do you think Paul would say to a young believer who asks him, "Who or what will help me to set my mind on Christ"?

THREE

We have died with Christ, been raised with Christ, have had our lives hidden with Christ in God, and will appear with Him in glory one day. That is our identity: we are in Christ. There is nothing more important about who we are than this—our being in Him. And all of this has happened to us "together" as members of Christ's body—His bride, the church.

The great togetherness of our Christian lives is going to be on full display in these following commands. Our moral character not only impacts us, but everyone around us. We do not live in a vacuum, but we exist in the context of the people around us.

READ THROUGH COLOSSIANS 3:5-11 THREE TIMES.

NOW READ THROUGH THE LIST OF "WHAT IS EARTHLY IN YOU" IN VERSE 5. HE'S GOING TO NAME THE SINS THAT DESTROY WHAT GOD LOVES.

Write down the sins Paul lists in the space below.

How does Paul summarize these things?

Because we are learning what life is like as part of God's new creation, we need to understand how our sin impacts the people around us. One way to fight temptation to sin is to imagine the ways that sin would affect the people in your life. Imagine yourself being caught in that sin. Imagine yourself confessing that sin to the people you love. How are they affected? What are the long-term effects on your life and theirs? How would your personal assurance of your participation in the new creation be affected after you willfully indulged in that sin?

Dealing with sin is deadly serious business, because it required the death of the perfect Son of God to atone for it, and sin means to kill us and cover the faces of those who are resurrected with shame.

How do you feel about naming the sins you struggle with? Are there some sins you would rather summarize as "things I'm struggling with" rather than summarize as "idolatry"? Explain.

Paul does not mince his words here. He says: "Put to death therefore" (v. 5). Why so drastic? Why is the apostle so adamant about killing sin? Believers in Christ should put these sins to death, because "with Christ you died to the elemental spirits of the world" (Col. 2:20). They are no longer still alive in the world and subject to such regulations and shadows.

> *The old has passed away; behold, the new has come.*
> **2 CORINTHIANS 5:17**

Why live as though you have not died to those things? Why walk like a zombie instead of in the newness of life in Christ? It makes no sense.

Also, there's Colossians 3:6, which says, "On account of these the wrath of God is coming." The idolatrous worship advocated by the false teachers is exposed as useless and damning. Only true worship—made possible by Christ and through Christ—is acceptable to our holy God. Remember that Paul has already said that his ministry encompasses both teaching and warning (Col. 1:28).

SLOWLY READ THROUGH VERSES 8-9.

Use these verses as a guide to confess your sin before God and repent. Not one of us is free from sin, so resist the urge to only see the faces of other people in your mind as you read the list. Rejoice that Colossians 3:5-11 comes after Colossians 1:1–3:4!

Why is it significant that Paul's exhortations to walk in the newness of life come after he reminds them of the gospel and who Christ is?

FOUR

Wasn't it wonderful to be reminded of the fact that Colossians 3:5-11 comes after Colossians 1:1–3:4? It seems like a rather elementary observation to make, but it is a crucial observation. Many people have lived their entire lives trying to live out the exhortations toward new creation life like the ones in the latter half of Colossians, yet they are not participating in God's new creation. In order to worship God like those who are in Christ in spirit and truth, we must first be placed in Christ. Then once we worship God rightly because of Christ in Colossians 1:15-20, we can understand ourselves to be circumcised in Him, baptized into His death, and raised to life with Him. And then once we understand who we are in Christ, then we understand who we are in relation to the church body, and our family, and those outside the church. But we are getting ahead of ourselves!

Colossians 3:9—and verse 8's "slander, and obscene talk"—deals directly with our speech.

What is the contrast between this kind of evil talk and "the word of the truth, the gospel" (Col. 1:5)?

What does Jesus teach concerning falsehood and lies (John 8:44)?

WE'VE ALREADY REFERRED TO 1 JOHN 1:5-10 IN THIS STUDY, BUT LET'S LOOK AT THAT PASSAGE ONE MORE TIME.

What do we learn about truth and the importance of speaking the truth?

The verb in Colossians 3:9 has connotations of disrobing. In a sense we are to take off the old self as though we would take off old clothes.

READ EPHESIANS 4:22-24.

How does this corresponding passage in Ephesians shed light on what Paul is talking about here?

What does Paul say in Colossians 3:10 concerning our new self?

What does he say is distinctive about the new self (you may also refer to Eph. 4:24)?

In the next Personal Study we will dig deeper into verses 10-11. For the remainder of your Personal Study time today, use the space below to reflect on what it means to continually be about "disrobing" the old self in your own life.

FIVE

Let's start our Personal Study today by reading Psalm 84.

PLEASE READ PSALM 84 AND MAKE IT YOUR PRAYER TODAY.

Verse 4 says, "Blessed are those who dwell in your house, ever singing your praise!" When we seek the things that are above, we are truly blessed. Even the sparrow finds a home. Don't you love that? Jesus assures us that we are certainly worth more than many sparrows (Matt. 10:31). We can enter God's dwelling place by the blood of Jesus, and now through Christ and the Spirit, God makes His home with us now. And a day is coming when we appear with Him in glory.

> *Behold, the dwelling place of God is with man. He will dwell with them, and they will be his people, and God himself will be with them as their God.*
> **REVELATION 21:3**

Amen. Come, Lord Jesus!

Until that day we put to death what is earthly in us, we seek the things that are above. We do not want to identify with those whose "end is destruction, their god is their belly, and they glory in their shame, with minds set on earthly things" (Phil. 3:19). That is not our story any longer now that we are in Christ!

We set our minds not to navel-gazing, dizzying rounds of fruitless introspection, or earthly things that pass away because they are perishable and temporary, but we set our minds on things that are above. We've been raised together with Christ. Our lives are now hidden with Christ in God. We "have put on the new self, which is being renewed in knowledge after the image of its creator" (Col. 3:10).

> *Where have we read about these concepts before? Think back over your study in Colossians, and write down in the space below where you have read about these subjects. (You can also refer to the whole Scripture, but please start looking in Colossians.)*

What is the new self?

What is happening to the new self?

In what likeness is the new self being renewed?

In Colossians 3:11 we read, "Here there is not Greek and Jew, circumcised and uncircumcised, barbarian, Scythian, slave, free; but Christ is all, and in all." Where have we read these denotations before? Again, starting in Colossians, make note of what you have read before about these things.

What is the difference between the new self in verse 10 and the worldly distinctions in verse 11?

TURN TO 1 CORINTHIANS 15:47-58 TO READ MORE ABOUT THE RESURRECTION WE WILL UNDERGO.

Paul contrasts the first man (Adam) and the second man (Jesus). Take notice of how verse 49 discusses image bearing: "Just as we have borne the image of the man of dust, we shall also bear the image of the man of heaven."

Write in the space below the contrasts in this passage between Adam and Jesus:

ADAM	JESUS
dust /earth flesh /blood mortal	heaven spirit immortal

What does this passage teach us about the relationship of sin, death, and the law?

Back in Colossians 3, we are told to "put to death therefore what is earthly in you" (v. 5), "put them all away" (v. 8), and "put off the old self" (v. 9). The reason we're given for this is in verses 9-10: "Do not lie to one another, seeing that you have put off the old self with its practices and have put on the new self, which is being renewed in knowledge after the image of its creator."

Again, we see Paul is arguing for believers to live consistently with the fact that they have died to sin and been raised together with Christ. We also recall from chapter 1 that all things were created by Christ and the new creation is His. So, we have put on the new [creation] self, but what does it look like?

What does it mean to be renewed in knowledge after the image of Christ?

In this broken, fallen world, the divisions of the old age (v. 11) still exist. What are the remnants of the old age divisions among humanity that you see in the world around you?

How are you affected by these divisions?

How does being placed in Christ encourage you even as you live in a world like the one you've described above?

Paul ends this part of his letter by saying, "but Christ is all, and in all" (v. 11b). Division belongs to the old age; unity belongs to the new age. We are all equals in Christ. In this age and in the next, Christ is all.

What comes to your mind when you hear the phrase "Christ is all"? Meditate on this passage of Scripture today, and use the space below to write down your reflections if you so desire.

GROUP TIME REVIEW

Let's begin by reviewing your Personal Study from the past week.

According to Colossians 3:1, who are the two persons who have been raised? In what ways were you aware or unaware of this teaching previously?

Me & Christ

What is the manner in which Christ will return and why? Who will appear with Christ on that day, and in what condition will they be in?

What does Paul mean when he exhorts the believers to seek the things that are above? How can you practically tell if you are seeking the things that are above?

What is the contrast between the evil speech patterns the Colossians are to put to death and the "word of the truth, the gospel" (Col. 1:5)?

In this broken, fallen world, the divisions of the old age still exist. What are the remnants of the old age divisions among humanity that you see in the world around you? How are you affected by these divisions?

DISCUSS VIDEO ON COLOSSIANS 3:1-11

What does it mean to be "renewed in knowledge" after the image of Christ (v. 10)?

The "togetherness" of being raised together (with Christ in His resurrection and with the church in her glorification) is a tremendous thought to meditate on. Using your Scripture-soaked imagination, what do you think you are most looking forward to when you recall that one day your body will be glorified together with the global church?

We can gain significant help when we are open to naming the specific sins with which we are troubled. Are there things that are part of the "old self" that cause you particular pain as you seek to put off the old self?

Colossians 3:11 says, "Here there is not Greek and Jew ... but Christ is all, and in all." How does this teaching of radical equality in Christ impact your heart today?

How can we pray for each other in terms of putting to death that which is earthly in us?

CLOSE

Get together in groups of two or more ladies and pray with one another, confessing your sin to the Lord and to one another, asking for God's help to walk in the newness of life that is yours in Christ.

SESSION 7:
COLOSSIANS 3:12–4:1

ONE

READ COLOSSIANS 3:12–4:1 THROUGH THREE TIMES. Make notes below of the themes and key words that stand out to you in this passage:

What is the command given in Colossians 3:12?

How does this command compare to the one given (and elaborated on) in Colossians 3:5-9?

Paul has written elsewhere about this putting off and putting on command. How do these passages in Ephesians shed light on Colossians 3:12?

Ephesians 4:24

Ephesians 6:11-15

In Colossians 3:12, Paul calls his readers "God's chosen ones, holy and beloved." This terminology has been used before, but it is used in reference to Israel.

Look up the following verses below, and describe who God's people are to be:

Exodus 19:5-6

Deuteronomy 7:6-8

How can Paul now call the Colossian believers by this special name—"God's chosen ones, holy and beloved" (Col. 3:12)?

TWO

This idea of calling is discussed in other places in Paul's letters, perhaps most notably in Ephesians 4:1. In the previous three chapters of Ephesians, Paul describes the gospel and Christ's ascension and exaltation, and in the second half of the letter (the last three chapters), Paul describes what it looks like to live in light of that all-encompassing reality.

> *READ EPHESIANS 4:1-3, AND ANSWER THE QUESTIONS BELOW.*
>
> *What is the connection between one's calling and one's conduct?*
>
>
>
> *How does this passage in Ephesians correspond to what we are learning in Colossians about "putting off" the old person and "putting on" the new?*

The apostle Peter has also written about this concept—that of being called, or chosen, by God and the conduct befitting those who are chosen.

> *Read 1 Peter 2:9, and write down words that describe our identity as God's people and our purpose.*

And finally, the apostle John, in his apocalyptic vision on Patmos, describes what he hears and sees, addressing the seven churches in Revelation 1:4-7.

> *Read this passage, and write down words that describe our identity as God's people and our purpose.*

Now, back to Colossians 3:12, what does Paul tell "God's chosen ones, holy and beloved" to "put on"? Make a list in the space below.

In our languages we have expressions that connect our emotional state to our physiology. In English one can describe their anxiety as "having butterflies in their stomach" or their great sadness as "having a broken heart." In Portuguese to talk about nervousness the expression is "cold in my belly." In Japanese someone can describe how they want something desperately and say "their hand comes from their throat." In Farsi, to tell someone how dear they are to you, tell them "you are my liver." In other non-Western languages, feelings of pain and fear are connected to the bowels (or "guts"). To use a biblical example, the literal rendering of Philippians 1:8 says that Paul greatly longs after the Philippians "in the bowels of Jesus Christ" (KJV). In this case in Colossians 3:12, to put on a "compassionate" heart would describe a feeling of sympathy that is so deep it comes from the gut level.

What is it like to feel a gut-level sympathy for someone? What do you want for that person, and with what intensity do you want it?

How does having a compassionate heart reflect the heart of Jesus? Give examples.

How does remembering that you are "God's chosen ... holy and beloved" child change the way you view the command to put on "compassionate hearts, kindness, humility, meekness, and patience"?

THREE

READ COLOSSIANS 3:12–4:1.

Going back to Colossians 3:13 we read, "bearing with one another and, if one has a complaint against another, forgiving each other; as the Lord has forgiven you, so you also must forgive." The connotation of the term "bearing with one another" carries the idea of enduring, persisting, and exercising patience. Admittedly, this does not sound like a fun command to obey.

How does this kind of conduct show forth the new self, "which is being renewed in knowledge after the image of its creator" (Col. 3:10)?

Further in verse 13 we learn about what forgiveness looks like for those who have put on the new self. Describe this kind of forgiveness in the space below:

Does this kind of forgiveness characterize the way you forgive others and your motive for doing so?

In verse 14, Paul says, "And above all these put on love, which binds everything together in perfect harmony." In keeping with the clothing metaphor, Paul is using (putting off and putting on), it seems that love could be a sort of binding belt, strap, or sash to hold everything together.

What do the following passages teach us about love?

Romans 13:8-10

1 Corinthians 13:1-13

Now in Colossians 3:15-16 we read about two "lets." These two "lets" are actually verbs in the Greek language, and direct translations into English read like this: "Peace of Christ let rule" and "word of Christ let dwell."

Digging into verses 15-16, what is "the peace of Christ"? What is "the word of Christ"?

Why do you think Paul is highlighting these two "lets"?

What is the result of the new self allowing these two "lets" to do their work in us—both as individuals and as a corporate body of Christ?

Peace of Christ

Word of Christ

Putting on the new self involves making these two our priorities. We have been given the peace of Christ, so we let it rule in our hearts. We have been given the word of Christ, so we let it dwell in us richly. It is notable that one cannot live out these two "lets" commands in isolation from other believers.

*JUST LOOKING AT VERSES 15-16, ANSWER THE FOLLOWING
QUESTIONS BELOW.*

What does "the peace of Christ" have to do with the church?

What does "the word of Christ" have to do with the church?

READ THE PARALLEL PASSAGE IN EPHESIANS 5:18-21.

*How does the flow of this passage mirror the one we have been looking
at in Colossians 3?*

These are some hard-hitting, challenging verses, aren't they? All of us fall short
of God's holy perfection, but praise God, our righteousness before Him does
not come from us. It comes from Christ! We can rest in the fact that Christ's
righteousness is imputed to us by faith, and with hearts overflowing with
thankfulness to God for all things, we can seek to put on the new self and
reflect His image.

FOUR

Today we are looking at a summary statement that encompasses everything about the way we live as we put off the old self and put on the new self. Let's look closer at verse 17:

And whatever you do, in word or deed, do everything in the name of the Lord Jesus, giving thanks to God the Father through him.
COLOSSIANS 3:17

The first phrase "whatever you do" is clarified by two categories. What are they?

The term "everything" in this passage literally means everything. Does Paul exclude anything in this command? (This is not a trick question—just want to make sure we're still tracking with the perspicuity of the text.)

To invoke someone's name is a way of summarizing everything that person is and represents. Use some Colossian terminology, and write a brief summary of the Lord Jesus. Who is He, and what is He about?

What is the church's motive in conducting herself (in word and deed) "in the name of the Lord Jesus"? What role does thankfulness play in this motive?

READ 1 CORINTHIANS 10:31-33.

What does Paul say is his personal motive for conducting himself with the Lord Jesus in mind? How does this perspective challenge you personally?

Is it possible to "do everything in the name of the Lord Jesus" (Col. 3:17)? What would you say to someone who is utterly disheartened when they hear this verse because they know they are a sinful person?

A couple of days ago when we did Personal Study Three you may have noticed at the end how Paul is setting us up to consider our relationships with one another in the body of Christ. Both in Colossians 3 and in the parallel passage in Ephesians 5:18 and following, we are given instructions of our conduct as new creations in Christ, and then Paul spells out our relationships and how they are to be ordered in this new creation. We're not going to dive into that part today, but hold on tight—we're getting there tomorrow!

FIVE

This is one of my favorite aspects of studying Paul's letters to the various churches. Paul not only says things that challenge individuals to live in light of who they are (as individuals) in Christ, but he puts all of this in the perspective of us having been saved to be the bride of Christ, the church. Everything we are learning about the putting off of the old self and the putting on of the new self has to do with our corporate identity as the people of God. We—together—are raised with Christ, and so this is how we live together as His people who are members of one another.

"Put to death ... what is earthly in you" (Col. 3:5) refers not only to sinful actions but attitudes as well. Through the gospel Jesus has broken down every dividing wall among us. All of the conceit, pride, and ethnocentrism we experience in our everyday lives are part of the elements of the world. Such values belong to Satan and have no place in the church because we are part of the new creation in Christ. In this passage concerning the Christian household Paul addresses our "old self" relational tension head-on. He shows us what it looks like to live in light of the fact that Christ is on the center stage of the cosmos as God has made Him to be the head of all things.

READ COLOSSIANS 3:18–4:1 ONE MORE TIME.

Sketch an outline of the people whom Paul addresses in the space below:

We've been transferred out of the world—out of the kingdom of God's enemy—and into the kingdom of the Son, whom He loves. We have a new citizenship and a totally new (creation) life. The church is different than the world, and she ought to behave differently. When God called us and set us apart for Himself from before the foundation of the world, our future of being presented mature in Christ was certain. So when we live lives that are contrary to that future, then we are utterly rogue, inauthentic, and unfruitful.

Several times over in this passage, Paul refers to Jesus Christ the Lord. Jesus is the ultimate, cosmic household manager. He is Lord over all—putting the cosmos back together under His loving rule. The manner in which we live out the instructions for our familial relationships is according to the peace of Christ, which rules our hearts, and the word of Christ, which dwells in us richly. Ordered relationships and befitting conduct is how we participate in God's cosmic plan to order everything under Jesus' feet, as He is Head over all.

I do realize that the ideas of submission and obedience can conjure up dreadful feelings in those of us who have been subject to people abusing their authority in our lives. In this passage Paul does not elaborate on all of the "what ifs" that may come into our minds. No doubt, the first readers of this passage had some "what ifs" come to their minds, too! Let's see what the text does say.

In verse 18, who is addressed? And what is the significant explanation given in this verse?

What is "fitting in the Lord"? What is not fitting to Him?

In verse 19, who is addressed? What is the elaboration given in this verse? Why do you think Paul highlights this particular manifestation of the old self?

In verse 20, who is addressed? What is the enticing explanation given? Why is this people group included in this description of a household properly ordered under Christ?

In verse 21, who is addressed? What is the reason given?

In verses 22-25, who is addressed? What is the manner of service that Paul exhorts?

What is the motive given?

What does it mean to be a people-pleaser?

Who is addressed in Colossians 4:1? What is the command given? And the reason given for this command?

In any or all of these relationships, it is reasonable to think that some of us who are under authority might have reasons to be afraid. Bondservants are told to serve "with sincerity of heart, fearing the Lord" (3:22). We know that the fear of the Lord frees us from every other fear. But what if someone—a wife, husband, child, employee, or otherwise—is in danger because of the conduct of those who are in authority over them? We need God's help for these heartbreaking situations. Paul specifically warns that "the wrongdoer will be paid back for the wrong he has done, and there is no partiality" (3:25). We are assured of God's perfect justice. While we yet live in this fallen world under authorities who abuse and mistreat us, we need God's wisdom.

If you or someone you know are experiencing abuse (emotional, psychological, verbal, spiritual, sexual, or physical), pray that God would show you how to walk in wisdom as you seek help. I urge you to seek out help from trusted authorities, trusted church leaders, family members, or close friends. If your life or the life of your children are in danger, please seek refuge somewhere safe immediately. If you are in any of the aforementioned situations or are supporting someone who is, please visit this website to learn how to move forward: http://justinholcomb.com/making-a-safety-plan.

All of us—whether or not we are able to easily submit to godly authorities over us—can be supportive and prayerful for those in our midst who are suffering. We have a Master in heaven who sees everything, and it is to Him we look for our help and our hope. We trust Him with hearts full of faith that what He says is right and good, because He is right and good.

GROUP TIME REVIEW

Let's begin by reviewing your Personal Study from the past week.

What is the significance of Paul calling the Colossian believers by this special name—"God's chosen ones, holy and beloved" (Col. 3:12)?

How does love bind everything together as believers put on the new self?

What does it look like to personally "let the word of Christ dwell in you richly" (v. 16)? What does that look like practically for an individual in Christ? And for a local church?

Is it possible to "do everything in the name of the Lord Jesus" (v. 17)? What would you say to someone who is utterly disheartened when she hears this verse because she knows she is a sinful person?

What does it mean that a wife's submission is "fitting in the Lord" (v. 18)?

WATCH VIDEO ON COLOSSIANS 3:12–4:1

_____
_____
_____
_____
_____
_____
_____
_____
_____
_____
_____
_____
_____
_____
_____
_____
_____
_____
_____
_____
_____
_____
_____
_____
_____
_____
_____

DISCUSS VIDEO ON COLOSSIANS 3:12–4:1

What does it feel like to put off the old self and put on the new self? Is there any conflict going on? If so, what is that like?

Conduct flows from character, as they say. And it is true! God's people are being renewed in knowledge after the image of our Creator. All of the specific commands and warnings in this passage are descriptions of what the new humanity in Christ looks like. In what ways are you personally challenged by this passage?

Consider the reminder that "you also have a Master in heaven" (Col. 4:1). How does this remembrance affect the way you treat the people around you? Specifically, how does this fact affect how you consider people who serve you (hospitality industry, retail employees, coworkers, etc.)?

To whom is our service and submission directed in every instance and in every relationship? Why—what is the cosmic reason for this command?

Colossians was written to people who were tempted to trust other forms of religion for their spiritual growth and not trust fully and exclusively in Christ, in whom the fullness of deity dwells. As the Colossian believers looked around them and saw the new self at work, how should they have been encouraged in their faith in Christ?

CLOSE

We will close in prayer today. And in closing, let's prayerfully read through Colossians 3:12–4:1 together. Ask the Lord for eyes of faith to see the beauty of His Son and the brilliance of His gospel as He is making all things new. Pray for mercy for those who are victimized by corrupt authorities, and ask God to make you a defender and ally for anyone in need. Is anyone among you guilty of misusing the authority given to you in either provoking children or mistreating people? Pray for God's mercy as ladies are exhorted from Scripture to repent and seek forgiveness from God, who is rich in mercy.

SESSION 8:
COLOSSIANS
4:2-18

The prayer of the righteous avail much!

ONE

Welcome to your Personal Study for the week. This section of Colossians may be tempting to skip because it looks like a list of names of people we don't know, but we're going to pause and get to know them. In doing so, we'll learn more about who God is and what it is like to serve Him faithfully. To start off this section we're going to study a few more instructions before we get to the personal greetings.

READ COLOSSIANS 1:1-14, AND THEN READ COLOSSIANS 4:2-6 SEVERAL TIMES. As we near the end of Paul's Letter to the Colossians we're going to be referring back to the beginning as well.

According to Colossians 4:2, what is the manner in which we are to pray?

watchful + thankful

How does Paul describe his prayers for the believers in Colossians 1:9?

Continually praying, filled them w/ knowledge, wisdom understanding

Thankfulness is specific and directed to someone for something. In Paul's prayer for this church plant, he has prayed for their attitude of gratitude.

Look up Colossians 1:11-14, and describe this thankfulness he asked God to work in their hearts.

endurance + patience

notes from Prayer on Saturday

To whom is our thankfulness directed, and why?

God, gives wisdom

What specific prayer request for himself and his colleagues does Paul share in Colossians 4:3-4?

Open up opportunities to share the Gospel in a clear simple manner

An open door does not necessarily refer to a physical door but to an opportunity.

What is the opportunity Paul is seeking?

What is the "word" to which Paul is referring (v. 3)? Look back to the beginning of his letter in Colossians 1:5-6.

Read about other open doors in the New Testament. What were these open doors like? Who opens these doors? Write your notes below.

Acts 14:24-28

1 Corinthians 16:5-9

2 Corinthians 2:12-13

Revelation 3:7-8

After Paul shares his prayer request concerning opportunities for the word in Colossians 4:3-4, he gives the Colossians instructions on how to avail of the opportunities that they are given for the word:

> Walk in wisdom toward outsiders, making the best use of the time.
> Let your speech always be gracious, seasoned with salt, so that you
> may know how you ought to answer each person.
> COLOSSIANS 4:5-6

What does it mean to walk in wisdom?

God's definition not ours.

RECALL THAT WISDOM IS A MAJOR THEME IN THIS LETTER. Look up the following verses to determine the kind of wisdom to which Paul is referring:

In Colossians 1:9, Paul prays that they may be filled with the knowledge of God's will in: *wisdom + understanding that the Spirit gives*

In Colossians 1:28, Paul says his ministry of proclamation involves warning and teaching everyone with: *all wisdom*

In Colossians 2:3, Paul says that in Christ are hidden all the treasures of: *wisdom and knowledge*

In Colossians 2:23, Paul warns about false teachers and their doctrine, saying they have only the appearance of: *wisdom*

In Colossians 3:16, as the word of Christ dwells in the Colossians richly, they are to teach and admonish one another in: *wisdom*

Paul describes how to walk in wisdom in the other circular letter that he sent along with Tychicus. Read Ephesians 5:15-17, and write your observations in the space below.

"be wise. understand God's will, not foolishness

A similar passage is found in 1 Thessalonians 4:11-12. Read this passage, and write down your observations about walking in wisdom toward outsiders.

We have a problem: we lack wisdom. Where can we get the wisdom
we need so that we may walk in it toward outsiders? Read the following
passages and make a note of where we can gain wisdom.

Proverbs 1:7

God's word
Holy Spirit
wise counsel

Colossians 1:9

Colossians 1:28

Colossians 2:3

James 1:5

<u>Wisdom is crucial to our witness to the gospel.</u> <u>Our gospel walk needs to match</u>
<u>up to our gospel words.</u> This is what it means to live consistently with the word
of truth we have been taught. Living sincere lives is not only important for us, but
also for our non-believing friends and family.

Looking back in Colossians 4:5-6, why do we need to walk in wisdom?

* Outsiders are watching

Why should our speech be gracious and seasoned with salt?

* ambassadors of Christ

Why is it important that our walking in wisdom precedes our talking?

. see a sermon
. people see you that will never talk to ym

Close your Personal Study this morning by asking for God to open doors for
you to speak the word of Christ, the gospel. Pray also that He would give you
the discernment you need to recognize the open doors and boldness to walk
through them.

TWO

Not even the apostle Paul could serve Jesus on his own. For the next three Personal Studies we're going to look at a passage in which Paul names, commends, and gives instructions regarding his colleagues—his fellow bondservants of Christ. This passage is a rather lengthy portion of personalized text compared to other letters we have from Paul. Romans is perhaps the only other letter that compares with this one in terms of length and personal commendations of Paul's co-laborers in the gospel.

LET'S DIVE RIGHT IN TO COLOSSIANS 4:7-17.

Read over this passage several times, and make a list below of the names mentioned. Make a note of where these people are from or where they live.

NAME	WHERE THEY'RE FROM/WHERE THEY LIVE
Tychicus	w/ Paul Colossae
Onesimus	↓
Aristarchus	Prison w/ Paul
Mark (Jew)	
Jesus (Justus) Jew	
Epaphras (Christ)	
Luke (doctor)	
Demas	
Nympha ~~at Laodicea~~ (house church)	Laodicea
Archippus	

In verses 7-8 we read about Tychicus. There are actually several places in the New Testament where we hear about this friend of Paul. Look up the following verses below, and write down what you are able to learn about Tychicus. Remember to look at the surrounding verses for context if something isn't quite clear.

Colossians 4:7-8

Acts 20:4

Ephesians 6:21

2 Timothy 4:12 (Note: To find out why Paul is doing this, read 2 Tim. 4:9,21.)

Titus 3:12 (Note: Paul is requesting Pastor Titus to leave Crete to visit him.)

In verse 9 we read about Onesimus, a member of the church in Colossae and the subject of Paul's Letter to Philemon.

READ PAUL'S LETTER TO PHILEMON ONCE THROUGH. *(It's only 25 verses.)*

What do you learn about Onesimus from Paul's Letter to Philemon?

How does Paul describe Onesimus in Colossians 4:9, which is addressed to the whole church at Colossae?

In verse 10 two men are mentioned: Aristarchus and Mark, the cousin of Barnabas. Aristarchus is mentioned many times, as he traveled with Paul several places. Most theologians agree that this is the same John Mark mentioned throughout Acts and Paul's letters and is the same John Mark over whom a dispute arose between Barnabas and Paul.

Read the following passages concerning Aristarchus, and look for clues that tell us more about him. Remember to look at surrounding verses for context if it isn't immediately clear.

Acts 19:29

Acts 20:4

Acts 27:2

Colossians 4:10

Philemon 24

And now we get to Mark, the cousin of Barnabas (aka, "John whose other name is Mark"). We'll read one set of verses first that describe how Mark started out in ministry and then after an incident in which he left the team and became the subject of a sharp disagreement between his cousin Barnabas and the apostle Paul.

What do you learn about him from these verses?

Acts 12:12,25

Acts 13:5,13-14

Acts 15:37-40

Now let's read a different set of verses. If that first set of verses describe a "before" picture, then this set of verses is like an "after" picture. What do you learn about Mark from these verses below?

Colossians 4:10

2 Timothy 4:11

Philemon 24

1 Peter 5:13

It is deeply encouraging to consider that Mark's past record of failure did not totally disqualify him from usefulness in ministry later on. It is believed that Peter took Mark under his wing, so to speak, and encouraged him to grow and mature in Christ. Peter, of course, knew what it was like to be redeemed from his failures!

How does this testimony of Mark's life encourage your faith?

In Colossians 4:11 we read about a man named Jesus, who is called Justus. Imagine! What a namesake. The name "Justus" literally means "*just*" or "righteous."

What does this nickname tell you about this companion of Paul's?

What is the meaning of his description as a man "of the circumcision"?

THREE

And now we are back to Epaphras, the man responsible for bringing the gospel to Colossae after he learned it from Paul in Ephesus. Let's go over what we know about Epaphras one more time.

Look up the verses below, and write down your observations about him.

Colossians 1:7

Colossians 4:12-13

Philemon 23

Epaphras was an evangelist to his own people, and apparently he took this role quite seriously. Paul mentioned a few things that were distinctive about Epaphras and his ministry. His faithfulness to the gospel, his fervent prayer life, and his dedication to serving alongside Paul to the point where he is named a "fellow prisoner in Christ Jesus" (Philem. 23).

Do you know any dear sisters or brothers who resemble Epaphras in their commitment to the gospel, to prayer, and to sacrificial service? What do you think motivates these dear ones?

What do you think motivates Epaphras?

Does your heart break for the people in your life who do not yet know Christ? What encouragement can you take from Epaphras's life and example of reaching his loved ones?

In verse 14 we read about two more men: Luke, the beloved physician, and Demas. We'll read more about both of these men, as they both have quite a history with Paul. First up is Luke. He is the author of two books in the New Testament—Luke and Acts. We also know he is a physician who accompanied Paul on his journeys as his personal doctor. In our previous Personal Study we read that Luke was with Paul at the end of his earthly life: "Luke alone is with me" (2 Tim. 4:11). Luke is the picture of faithful ministry to Christ and loyalty to Paul even through dangerous circumstances. Demas, however, seems to be the opposite.

Read the following verses, and make notes of what you learn about Demas.

Colossians 4:14

2 Timothy 4:10

Philemon 23-24

What happened to Demas? He went from being named as a fellow worker to a deserter. The text in 2 Timothy 4:10 says Demas loved this present *aion*—this present world—and so he abandoned Paul. Look at the wider context of 2 Timothy 4:9-18, which are some of the very last words we have from Paul, as he is near the end of his earthly life.

What does this situation seem like?

We do not know whether or not Demas ever repented. It may be that he did, but we do not have any record of this in Scripture. In the absence of such a conclusion either way, what admonition can we receive from this account of Demas's life?

How are you personally encouraged and warned by these two different examples of men who served alongside Paul?

FOUR

Read Colossians 4:7-18 one more time. Reading through this list of personal greetings and commendations, one gets the sense that Paul is a most appreciative friend and fellow minister of the gospel! I think Paul shared his ministry not only because he needed practical help in evangelizing, discipling, and traveling, but because this is the way Christian ministry was modeled to us by the Lord Jesus. It is right and fitting that a servant of Christ Jesus serves in the manner in which the Lord serves—through a body of believers.

READ IN COLOSSIANS 4:15-16 ABOUT SOME CHURCH PLANTS.

What do these verses teach us about how the early church operated?

And how they regarded apostolic letters, such as Colossians?

In his shout-out to Archippus, Paul gives him a very straightforward instruction that carries a significant reminder of authority. At least part of Archippus's ministry was as a co-host of a church, and we don't know whether or not he was discouraged or flagging in his zeal (thus prompting Paul to give this instruction). Archippus gets a mention in the Letter to Philemon in verse 2 as "our fellow soldier."

READ COLOSSIANS 4:17.

What do we know about Archippus's ministry from this verse? What is the significance of receiving a ministry in the Lord?

At last, at the very end of his letter, Paul gives his final greeting, exhortation, and blessing. Verse 18 reads:

I, Paul, write this greeting with my own hand. Remember my chains. Grace be with you.
COLOSSIANS 4:18

Reflecting on this entire list of names, greetings, and commendations, what can you learn from Paul's example of including others in your ministry?

In the face of great adversity, hard work characterized so many of the co-laborers whom Paul mentioned.

What are the biggest challenges you personally face when it comes to working hard in ministry and in remaining faithful during adversity?

Archippus the fellow soldier needed encouragement to serve. So do we! Add your own name here:

"Say to _____, 'See that you fulfill the ministry that you have received in the Lord.'"

What is the ministry you have been given by the Lord?

Paul's chains are gone and he has died. We recall his chains and how he was a prisoner for Christ so that we might know the grace of the Lord Jesus Christ. And we labor to remember the words he wrote that were carried along by the Holy Spirit. *Thank You, Father, for sustaining and persevering this brother to the very end so that we might know Your gospel and be raised together with Christ.* Paul's life is still hidden with Christ in God, and when Christ, who is his life, appears, then he also will appear with Him in glory.

Grace be with you.

FIVE

On this final day of Personal Study, read through the whole letter of Colossians, thanking God for what He has taught you in His Word. You can use the space below to write down any thoughts or reflections.

GROUP TIME REVIEW

Let's begin by reviewing your Personal Study from the past week.

Paul is in chains in jail. But for what kind of opportunity does Paul want the Colossians to pray for him? Why? What can we learn from this prayer request?

What does it mean to "walk in wisdom" according to Colossians 4:5?

Paul is sharing greetings and commendations from his fellow servants of Christ—fellow prisoners with him. What do Onesimus and Mark, the cousin of Barnabas (aka John Mark) have in common with each other? What do they have in common with you?

Epaphras is away from his hometown and the friends he won to Christ, and now false teachers are threatening the spiritual health of that young church plant. How does Paul's commendation of Epaphras at the end of Colossians help reinforce to the Colossians that they have received the true, full gospel?

Archippus was exhorted to see to it that he fulfills the ministry he received in the Lord. What does it mean for you personally to see to it that you fulfill your ministry? What role do others have in your ministry? Who are the people around you whom you could call fellow prisoners and fellow servants?

WATCH VIDEO ON COLOSSIANS 4:2-18

DISCUSS VIDEO ON COLOSSIANS 4:2-18

How do you define "prayer"? What is your prayer life like?

Is there something you have been praying for a long time? What encourages you to keep praying?

What have you learned in Colossians that emboldens you to pray to God?

What have you learned in Colossians that emboldens you to share the gospel with the lost?

Describe an opportunity you have experienced in which it was obvious that God had opened a door for His Word.

PULL UP A CHAIR.

Drop by the LifeWay Women blog to grow in your faith, develop as a leader, and find encouragement as you go. Find inside info on Bible studies, events near you, giveaways, and more at

LIFEWAYWOMEN.COM

AM I
JUST A MOM?

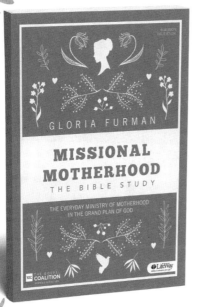

Sooner or later, every mother will stop and ask herself, *Is this all I am?*

God has instilled motherhood with meaning and purpose as part of His greater plan for humanity. Whether or not a woman has been called to traditional motherhood, she demonstrates her nurturing gifts daily through caregiving, hospitality, discipleship, teaching, raising children, and serving others.

Join Gloria Furman in this 6-session Bible study as she looks to Scripture for evidence of God's mission for motherhood and His greater purpose for each and every woman.

Bible Study Book   006101512 $12.99
Leader Kit   006101513 $69.99

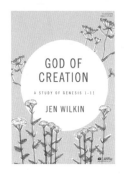

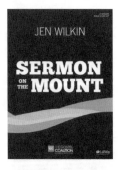